THE ROYAL HORTIC
PRACTICA

D0245928

SMALL
GARDENS

THE ROYAL HORTICULTURAL SOCIETY
PRACTICAL GUIDES

SMALL
GARDENS

JOHN MORELAND

DORLING KINDERSLEY
LONDON • NEW YORK • SYDNEY • MOSCOW
www.dk.com

LONDON, NEW YORK, MUNICH, MELBOURNE, DELHI

SERIES EDITOR Pamela Brown
SERIES ART EDITOR Stephen Josland
ART EDITOR Rachael Parfitt

MANAGING EDITOR Louise Abbott
MANAGING ART EDITOR Lee Griffiths

ILLUSTRATIONS Gill Tomblin

DTP DESIGNER Matthew Greenfield

PRODUCTION Ruth Charlton, Mandy Inness

First published in Great Britain in 1999
Reprinted 2003
by Dorling Kindersley Limited,
80 Strand, London WC2R 0RL

A Penguin Company

A CIP catalogue for this book is available from the British Library.
ISBN 0 7513 48635

Reproduced by Colourscan, Singapore
Printed and bound by Star Standard Industries, Singapore

See our complete catalogue at
www.dk.com

CONTENTS

DESIGNING A SMALL GARDEN 7

Deciding what you want of your
garden and how to achieve it. Assessing the site's
good points and bad points and the design solutions
that will help to transform it.

TWENTY SMALL GARDEN PLANS 30

A wide-ranging selection of 20 illustrated designs,
chosen to make the most of all kinds of sites and to suit
all sorts of needs. The plans show how to make
small spaces seem larger, accommodate changes of level,
as well as incorporate sitting and dining areas,
built-in barbecues, play areas, pools and pergolas and
a variety of other features.

BASIC DESIGN TECHNIQUES 72

Taking the right measurements, putting your plan onto
paper and then setting it out in the garden.

DESIGNING A SMALL GARDEN

WHAT ARE THE OPTIONS?

NO MATTER HOW SMALL a garden may be, in today's hectic world it can play an invaluable role – a retreat from the everyday stresses of life, somewhere to relax and recharge your batteries. A garden can make the ideal place to eat and to entertain friends, or allow the children to let off steam. The ideas and designs on the following pages show the very different ways in which you can make the most of your outdoor space and transform it into your perfect garden.

THE QUESTIONS TO ASK

There are two fundamental questions that you need to ask right at the start – "What have I got?"and "What do I want?" The first involves the hard facts about the garden – its size, shape, amount of sun or shade, seclusion or lack of it – and the second exactly how you intend to use it. The two lists of answers can then be woven into a harmonious, workable design. Choices will inevitably be tempered by what you can afford, and how much of the work, especially the hard-landscaping, you want to tackle yourself. Don't underestimate the time it will take. Decide too whether you want to carry out the design all in one go, both building work and planting, or whether you would prefer to do it in stages, over a period of time. Whatever you choose, it helps to have a masterplan that everyone involved accepts and can work to, however long the whole project takes.

PATTERN OF LEAVES
Lightly shaded gardens are fortunate in that they suit some of the most handsome foliage plants. Ferns and variegated shrubs bring life and vitality to the area around a small tree.

◄ A QUIET SPACE *In a small garden, it is easy to create an atmosphere of peace and tranquillity.*

ANSWERING YOUR NEEDS

For a design to be successful, it must suit the needs of all who use it, so decide at the start just what these are. You may want a garden that you can enjoy without having to spend a lot of time maintaining it (*see p.46*). For a family with children and pets, the demands will be greater, especially when it comes to storing bikes and toys and providing space for play (*see p.52*). Whatever your requirements, take time to decide. Make a list that everyone in the household can contribute to. It is better to take in all the demands at this stage than have to add them in later.

The extent of your interest in gardening – how much you enjoy tending plants and how much time you have to look after your garden, or possibly how much you want to avoid it – is crucial. The planting is an essential part of any garden, it creates its atmosphere. But in a very limited space you may have to choose between giving room to plants or a dining area. For a keen gardener, this can be the toughest decision of all. The importance of a dining area, and possibly a built-in barbecue, will affect the amount of hard-landscaping, and whether you need to create some overhead shade. Your list should make you decide if you need a shed (*see p.28*), space for a dustbin and washing line. How important is a lawn, pool (*see p.16*) or pergola? Do you want to grow herbs or vegetables, and do you need a greenhouse? Once you have the answers, you can start thinking about the design.

MEETING THE
CHALLENGE
At first glance, this neglected tangle of rubbish and weeds seems to highlight all the problems of a small urban garden – overlooked by flats that also block some of its light, a dustbin and washing line on permanent display and a boundary fence that seems to be its main feature. But it is not cause for despair. Once priorities for how to use the space have been decided, good design strategies will help to overcome its physical drawbacks (see pp.31–71), turning it into an attractive and desirable garden.

ASSESSING THE SITE

If you are starting a garden from scratch – for instance, if you have just moved into a newly built house and are faced with a bare patch of soil and equally bare fence – the

> ### Since every centimetre is precious, it is worth drawing an accurate plan

difficult part is often choosing from all the possibilities. If you have acquired an existing garden, it is worth allowing time, up to a year, to see what it offers, what you want to keep, especially which plants, and what you want to change. Alternatively

you may have a garden that you have lived with for several years. It has gradually evolved rather than being planned, but now you recognize it's really not what you want. Whichever scenario, draw up a checklist and a plan (see pp.72–75). Take accurate measurements of boundaries, changes in level and existing garages and sheds; note the direction of the sun, prevailing winds and good and bad views, and mark areas of paving and walling, also plantings, especially of shrubs and trees. The views from house windows are important, so mark these on the plan and take them into account in your design. In a newly built house, you may have to assess the state of the soil, whether it hides builders' rubble and if more good-quality topsoil needs to be imported.

PERFECT RESULTS
A carefully designed garden illustrates what can be achieved in a typical small city space (not much different from the one opposite). Paving is balanced by the plants, chosen for both leaf shape and foliage texture as well as their flowers. A white-painted wall reflects light, helping to improve plant growth, while a boundary clothed with climbers helps bring a feeling of seclusion. Globes of clipped box introduce a sense of order, and a coat of colour turns a functional watering can into a decorative feature.

CHOOSING A STYLE

NO MATTER HOW SMALL your garden is, before you start planning it in detail you need a clear picture in your mind of how you want it to look – the sort of atmosphere you want to create. Do you like clear lines and modern materials? Would you prefer a romantic profusion of plants? Or do you seek the orderly calm of a formal design? The choice of a style that you like and can translate into your garden space is one of your first, most important decisions.

SOURCES OF INSPIRATION

If you are lucky you may turn the page of a magazine or book and see just the sort of garden you want. If so, it's important to hold the picture in your mind's eye as you start putting your design into practice. More often, though, it's not quite as simple as that, and you need to take time seeking ideas from as many sources as possible. Glean inspiration from photographs and TV programmes, and see what pleases you in other people's gardens. Even if they are on a very much larger scale, gardens that are open to the public may have corners or areas that can be copied or adapted. Keep an open mind until your ideal style starts to emerge, then be ready to discard anything that does not obviously fit in.

TIME AND PLACE

Though you may not consciously want to choose a historical model, there are few styles that have not been put into practice at some time in the past. If you like formal designs, there is plenty to be learned from the symmetry and patterns found in the grand gardens of stately homes. Knot gardens, for instance, are easily translated

PLANT PARADISE
The owner of this garden clearly likes plants and – with careful choice of flower colour and leaf shape – has created an oasis in a small, enclosed urban area. It is satisfying to all the senses, but will require time and attention on a continuing basis.

◄MODERN TWIST
*Here, glass blocks
have been used both
for paving and to
form a boundary
screen. It would be
easy to create
marvellous night-time
effects by lighting up
different sections of
the paved area.*

▼ LONG TRADITIONS
*A conventional
mixture of lawn
and shrubs produces
an easy atmosphere,
and looking after it
should not be too
burdensome. A
secluded area has
been created by
dividing the garden's
length with a screen
(see p.32).*

to a smaller scale, though they need a high
level of maintenance. And though the
cottage-garden style looks deceptively
simple, as if it has emerged naturally, in
reality it usually needs the regular attention
of a keen gardener. It is not essential to
stick to one style. Some of the most
successful gardens use a combination. An
informal, romantic mixture of plants may
billow within the confines of a precisely
clipped hedge. Large gardens divided into
"rooms" are a useful source of good ideas.

You may want to draw on the traditional
gardens of other countries. The raked
gravel and constrained planting of Japanese
design fit well into a pocket-sized space.
In an enclosed space, a Moorish-style
courtyard might be appropriate.

Large garden exhibitions and shows, such
as the Chelsea Flower Show in London
each year, are the best place to see modern
designs, spot the latest trends and discover
how new or unusual materials can be used.

SUITING YOUR LIFESTYLE

IT IS IMPORTANT THAT YOUR GARDEN serves you and that you do not feel a slave to your garden. After a hard day's work, the last thing you want is to spend time mowing the lawn or clipping a hedge. Alternatively, gardening may be just the hobby you seek – tending to plants, even weeding, is absorbing and therapeutic. Whatever your requirements, make sure that your design not only looks good but also suits you and your family's needs and way of life.

KEEPING MAINTENANCE LOW

For the majority of designers, this is the most common request of all. Most keen gardeners will say that a truly low maintenance garden is an impossibility, that where nature and plants are involved an element of care will always be essential. But it is possible to design a garden that can be managed with a minimum of maintenance. It is a matter of balancing the amount of hard surfacing against the "soft" planted areas that need regular care. The amount of care needed depends directly on the sort of planting you choose. Closely grouped flowering shrubs require little routine attention once established, except for occasional pruning. Borders full of annuals and perennials, on the other hand, need dedicated time and effort. The inclusion of

> There are plenty of less labour-intensive alternatives to lawns

a lawn may be a major consideration. Will its size warrant the effort needed to look after it? There are plenty of alternatives (*see p.24 and the plans from p.32 on*).

OUTDOOR ROOM
A secluded dining area makes an inviting place to enjoy an early morning coffee or entertain friends to a full-blown dinner party. The colour of garden furniture and other structures is important in the overall effect. Here, it has been kept to a minimum, with the same muted shade used for trellis, arch and table and chairs.

THE OUTDOOR LIFE

Increasingly people are using their garden as a place to eat and to entertain. You can either include a purpose-designed area with built-in furniture or, more simply, provide space to bring out chairs and a table when the mood strikes you. Make sure there is enough room for people to sit comfortably and move back from the table without disappearing into the undergrowth!

Siting a regular dining area is important – it usually needs to be within easy reach of the kitchen, and most people prefer to sit in dappled shade. Make use of existing trees or erect overhead beams that can be used to support climbers (*see pp.54 and 63*).

WELCOME GLOW
Candles, protected by coloured shades, create an intimate, relaxed atmosphere among a leafy planting of ivy and ferns.

Lighting will extend the ways you can use the garden – today's technology will help you to conjure up wonderful moods and effects (*see p.55*). If you want to run electricity to a patio, decide at the outset so that the conduit can be safely laid under paving. It is also worth deciding how often you want to use a barbecue, and whether a built-in barbecue should be part of the plan. If so, where space is at a premium, include some storage in its design.

COOK'S CORNER
With the walls of a built-in barbecue providing planting pockets for small herbs, plus a well-stocked herb patch nearby, the cook in this garden has a wealth of flavourings close to hand.

THE FAMILY'S NEEDS

I N A FAMILY GARDEN the changing needs and safety of children are paramount, and, if you accommodate these, it is far more likely that your garden – and your temper – will survive intact. Much grief is generated if children feel they have nowhere to play freely without being chastised. Once they reach a suitable age, give them their own space if you can, screening it with plants or trellis.

CHANGING NEEDS

Since a small garden is limited in what it can accommodate, it is important to consider the family's immediate needs and how these are likely to change in the coming years. Small children are usually easily catered for with an area of hard surfacing where they can pedal and wheel toys, and a small sandpit which will give them hours of absorbed pleasure. The play area needs to be close to and visible from the house at all times. Movable sandpits or paddling pools may be the answer. The garden's design must be practical – with somewhere to store bikes and toys – and above all safe

(*see opposite*). Avoid having paths of gravel that can cause cuts and grazes, and which small children can never resist scattering.

As the children grow, so does the need for a space where they can play ball games and enjoy more stimulating physical activity. If you have room for an adventure playground (*see p.52*), with slide, climbing frame and even a play-house, it will help to take the pressure off other parts of the garden. Play-bark, washed sand or smooth pea-shingle make an ideal safety surface. Remove the top layer of soil and lay a geotextile membrane (available from builders' merchants and garden centres),

▲ PUT THE LID ON
A wooden cover protects a sandpit when not in use but when slid aside can form part of the play area.

▶ LOOKING AHEAD
A decoratively shaped sandpit has been designed with the future in mind. In later years it could be lined and turned into a water feature or filled with topsoil and planted.

PLAY APPEAL
A robust but friendly looking wooden swing not only invites play but makes a harmonious feature in the garden. Make sure that supporting posts are absolutely secure. Installing play structures like this may be best left to the professionals. The low border of shrubs will be able to withstand the occasional, but inevitable, wildly aimed ball.

anchoring it into the ground with strong wire pegs. Fill in the area with bark, sand or shingle to a depth of at least 30cm.

THE SACRED TURF

It is important to ensure that you select an appropriate, hard-wearing grass seed mix if a lawn is to be used for ball games and more vulnerable the grass will be to wear and tear. Soft-stemmed herbaceous plants are easily battered, so be realistic and opt instead for tough shrubs to plant in surrounding borders. And if children show signs of interest in gardening, encourage them with their own tiny patch of easy plants such as sunflowers or candytuft.

> Grass is most easily damaged if it is played on while still wet

general play. Take advice from your garden centre and choose one of the tougher mixes, usually known as an "amenity" mix. After sowing in spring or autumn, give the lawn a fighting chance to develop into a good, resilient surface before allowing a ball anywhere near it. Remember that the smaller the area, the

SAFETY AND PLAY

- Give a sandpit a removable cover to prevent pets from fouling it, and use only washed or silver sand to avoid staining.
- If using bark, choose play-bark; ordinary chipped bark can splinter and cause injury. (Animals may also be attracted to bark.)
- Avoid spiny plants, such as yuccas, those that can irritate skin, such as rue, and poisonous plants, especially those with tempting berries and seedpods.
- Ensure water features are safe (*see p.17*).
- Put rubber caps on any bamboo canes.
- Ensure pots or statues cannot topple over.

EXTENDING PLANTING OPPORTUNITIES

IF YOU ARE A PLANT ENTHUSIAST you may well want to design in features that extend the range you can grow. Two of the best for small spaces are water features – for lush-leaved, moisture-loving plants – and raised beds – superb for letting plants trail or bringing them closer to the eye. Plan the features in at the start, siting pools carefully and organizing electric conduit before laying paving. You can use the topsoil from paving excavations to fill your raised beds.

PONDS, POOLS AND FOUNTAINS

Don't be put off the idea of a water feature because of fears that it will soon turn dank and disagreeable. There are some simple rules to follow (*see opposite*). It is important to choose a feature that fits in with the style of the garden. Whether raised or at ground level, a formal pool is usually symmetrical with clear, uncluttered edges that call for a careful choice of building material. The edges of informal pools look more naturalistic, often using different-sized shingle and blending gently into surrounding planting. Don't make the pool too small and don't let it become choked with plants. When choosing water plants, consult a book or reputable supplier so that you buy the most suitable, in the right quantity. In a tiny garden or courtyard,

Millstone or cobblestone fountains are safe for gardens with children

pools in waterproof half-barrels or frost-proof ceramic bowls are ideal. Bowls can also be set into decking (*see p.68*). Wall spouts, too, suit enclosed spaces (*see p.62*)

▲ HEAD ABOVE WATER
Small pools offer the opportunity to display a whimsical sense of humour.

► STILL WATERS
The feeling of serenity that pervades this formal moon-shaped pool is enhanced by the refreshing leafiness of the plants and a figure of a contemplative buddha.

BACK TO THE BED
Seats, with their own back-rests, can be built into raised beds, allowing you to sit and revive tired limbs surrounded by pleasant greenery.

but need electricity to work a pump, as do millstone and cobblestone fountains. This kind of moving water feature, with no exposed reservoir of water, is ideal if there are children. If you want a still pool where children have access, you should secure a strong metal grille just below the surface.

MAKING WATER WORK

- Site pools and ponds in open areas, away from shade and deciduous trees and shrubs.
- The pool area needs to be level.
- Line informal pools with polythene or butyl. Butyl costs more but lasts longer.
- Formal pools are easily made from dark-coloured pre-formed liners, or can also be built from waterproof, rendered brick or blockwork.
- Make sure that the pool's edge (whether of brick, paving slab, cobble or turf) has an overhang that casts a shadow and hides the liner.

ADDING A RAISED BED

Quite often in a small garden you want an area of paving and, after excavating, have plenty of surplus topsoil. Rather than removing it from the site, design in some raised planting areas, especially if it avoids having to carry soil through the house. Check that the amount of soil you dig out will be sufficient to fill the planned beds. Sizes can vary greatly according to whatever suits the design. As you excavate, keep topsoil and subsoil separate and add them to the beds in the correct order, making the layer of topsoil at least 45cm deep. As in any new planting area, it is important that drainage is good and that subsoil and any compacted soil are well broken up.

Raised beds extend the range of plants you can grow. Add grit to make soil more free-draining to suit most rock plants, also many herbs and Mediterranean plants, whose aromatic foliage will be brought all the closer. Using ericaceous compost will suit rhododendrons, heathers and other acid-loving plants. Not least, raised beds are the answer for anyone with a bad back or who has difficulty bending (see p.59).

ELEMENTS OF GOOD DESIGN

PROBABLY *THE* GOLDEN RULE of good design is that of simplicity. Too often gardens appear overly fussy, especially when a wide assortment of different hard materials have been used. Designing is, for the most part, about creating patterns and bringing together different elements. Wherever possible you should aim to achieve an overall sense of balance and harmony, unless of course you wish deliberately to introduce drama.

AREAS OF TRANSITION

Most garden designs start from the house, with a mix of planting and paving making the all-important link. As you move away from the house, the design becomes "softer", with the planting used to enclose the garden or frame good views beyond.

When drawing up your design, sometimes it helps to run out lines from doorways and windows so that you can incorporate visual links with areas of planting and paving. In a garden planned to include distinct, different areas or "garden rooms", consider how to encourage the desire to move between them. The plan on page 56 includes enticing elements of transition: hard paving by the house leads on to a sweep of lawn that in turn draws the eye to a narrow archway giving a glimpse of the "wild" garden beyond.

GUIDING PRINCIPLES
Statues can be used to guide a visitor along a meandering path, adding an element of mystery along the way. Giant pebbles make markers for the path edges.

BAY WATCH
It would be foolish to clutter a garden with distracting detail when it enjoys such a magnificent view. The wall offers shelter yet can be overlooked to keep sight of the bay.

◄PUTTING IT IN
PERSPECTIVE
*This garden, like the
one opposite, seems
to have an idyllic
view. In reality, a
carefully placed
mirror on the wall is
only reflecting the
garden itself. The pair
of conifers on either
side of the mirror and
its trellis frame,
designed to give
perspective to the
view, unite in
reinforcing the
illusion.*

PATTERN AND LINE

Inspiration does not always come from looking at other gardens; you may find it in far less likely sources. The design of a piece of jewellery, or a carpet or wallpaper pattern may suggest shapes for paving and beds – a knot garden, for instance – and a swatch of fabric may provide the colours for a planting scheme. Or, you may find an eye-catching piece of driftwood or sculpture and decide to build your whole design around that one element.

If you decide on an intricate pattern such as a knot garden, draw it up accurately, then set it out on the ground to check that it fits (*as shown on p.77*). Where the design is less formal and composed of sweeping curves, draw true circles (using a pair of compasses), ensuring that each curve links into the other.

THE GOLDEN RULES

• Keep the design simple.

• Keep the range of hard materials for surfaces, boundaries and any other features to a minimum.

• Where paving, such as brick, links house and garden, if possible use materials that match the house.

• Run out design lines and axes from the centres of doorways and windows.

• Consider how you will move from one area to another, and whether features such as archways or pergolas, statues or sculpture would help to draw you on.

• Try to create a feeling of mystery and surprise.

• Use your planting to soften and enclose, or to frame or focus attention on views that lie beyond the boundary.

• Make a definite choice between harmony and drama.

ON THE BOUNDARY

A GARDEN'S BOUNDARIES can be one of its most problematic areas. Where necessary, introduce changes right at the start. If you are lucky enough to have a garden enclosed by lovely old walls, you will want them to be a key element in your design. But all too often what you are faced with is a fence of larch-lap panels that have been stained a glaring shade of orange.

CARE WITH COLOUR

When you walk into a garden with bare, exposed fences, your eye is taken straight to its edges, foreshortening the space and making it feel distinctly smaller. The secret, wherever possible, is to "lose" the boundary. The fastest and simplest way is with colour. If the fencing is pale or bright, light is reflected, making the fence stand out all the more. By painting or staining it a darker shade, you will find that the boundary recedes and blends in. There is an ever-increasing range of good weather-proof preservatives available today in the darker colours. Look for blacks, dark browns and subtle tones of blue and green.

CHANGING PERCEPTIONS

Planting is another excellent way of concealing the garden's edge (*see the plan on p.36*). If necessary, change the colour of the fence first to improve its looks while

▲ FRAGRANT FENCE
If you don't want to block out the view, trellis makes a light, airy perimeter and will support climbers such as honeysuckle.

◀ BAMBOOZLED
Really thick planting will obscure the boundary completely. Bamboos can be invasive, but are good mufflers of noise while providing their own soothing rustle.

▲HIGH POINT
*A cleverly designed trellis
helps to raise the height of the
boundary in chosen places, to
screen unwanted views.*

◀TIME FOR TRELLIS
*Fix trellis to a wall before
planting the climbers that it
is to support. The job is twice
as difficult once the plants
are growing.*

the plants grow. It is important, too, when designing the plan, to allow sufficient space for the plants to form a good deep border to screen out the fence. Most shrubs need to spread to at least a metre; really luxuriant growers such as fatsias will spread to about three metres, and many bamboos as far as you let them. If space is tight, a profusion of climbers should do the trick. When well chosen and fully grown, the plants will prevent you from seeing where the garden ends, creating the illusion of much greater overall size.

Most climbers and wall shrubs need some form of support. Trellis is often the neatest solution. If that, too, is bright orange, change it to a more muted colour. You can create interesting harmonies with the fence behind. Stain one a bluish-green, for instance, and the other a greenish-blue. The same goes for camouflaging ugly walls.

VIEW FROM THE OTHER SIDE

Some problems – or opportunities – may lie beyond the boundary. You may merely want to increase your sense of privacy. A thick planting or some trellis raised a little above the boundary is often enough. If there is an eyesore, hide it with tall plants at the appropriate point or use purpose-

> Don't let a good view go
> to waste: frame it with
> boundary plants

designed trellis. A carefully chosen tree may be the answer. In a small garden, a hedge of Leyland cypress is seldom the solution. It must be kept to a sensible height; if allowed to shade surrounding gardens, it can blight relations with the neighbours.

ILLUSIONS OF SPACE

ABOVE ALL ELSE, GARDEN DESIGN is about playing with space, and a major part of that is creating the illusion of greater space – either confusing the eye or leading it on from one area to another. By dividing a garden you can introduce an element of mystery and surprise, suggesting that what lies out of view is worth exploring. In a rectangular or square site, you can make a garden seem larger by swinging the axis around so that it lies at an angle to the house.

DIVERSIONARY TACTICS

Many, if not most, gardens are long and thin and, if the central area is left open, the eye is drawn straight to the back boundary. One way of adding interest and making the garden seem wider is to subdivide its length with screens that project in from the sides towards the centre (*see p.32*). These divert your gaze, so that although the end may still just be in view, you cannot see it all in one swift second. These dividing screens can be created by simply extending borders with some tall plantings. Alternatively you can introduce hedging – evergreen or deciduous, clipped or informal, to suit different styles – or trellis panels. These can, of course, be used to support plants. In winter, when the sun is low, a screen of trellis or poles will cast dramatic shadows on the ground around.

CLEVER SCREENS

• Evergreen hedging can be clipped into interesting shapes, or even given "windows" to offer a tantalizing glimpse beyond.

• Paint or stain trellising in attractive colours, or make it out of different materials such as bamboo.

• Use a line of scaffolding poles, cut to length, or timber poles, with or without their bark and stained or painted if you wish.

• Woven hazel or willow screens work well if they have a sufficiently open pattern. Or you can plant a row of willows and train them to form a lattice-work trellis.

GARDEN ROOMS

Another way to disguise length is to divide the garden into different areas with one leading through to the other via "doorways" created by pergolas or arches (*as in the plans on pp.42 and 44*). At a glance you

THE ENTIRE VIEW?
At first this garden appears open and complete, a symmetrically arranged rectangle of lawn and shrubs. But at the end it closes with a flight of steps, creating a sense of mystery and the desire to discover where they lead.

CHARMED CIRCLE
*A prettily planted
trellis acts as a screen,
projecting from one
side of the garden so
that you cannot see
the complete length.
But the cunningly
placed "window"
also gives you a view
of the area beyond.
This has been given
the perfect shape to
frame a tree in a
circular raised bed.*

can see one complete area but the doorway entices you on, to discover what happens beyond. Dividing a garden into different areas makes it easy to introduce different styles, such as "wild" areas (*see p.56*) and children's playgrounds (*see p.52*). It also makes it possible to put a new plan into action in several stages. Clipped hedges or panels of trellis can be given cleverly placed windows that offer a framed view of the "room" next door.

WORKING ON THE DIAGONAL

If you look at any rectangular or square area, the longest line that you can draw within it is neither its length nor width but its diagonal. So one way of creating a sense of greater space is to orientate your design at that angle (*as in the plans on pp.40, 54 and 68*). In a square garden the angle will obviously be 45°. If your garden is long and narrow, you could use two sets of 45° diagonal lines. This usually looks better than odd, narrow angles, especially if you are using square paving slabs or tiles, which look much better when cut in half along the diagonal. Cutting usually becomes necessary where paving meets the boundary or the house wall (*see p.40*).

Decking lends itself to this sort of design (*see p.68*) as the planks create directional lines; the effect of greater space can be further enhanced with the use of mirrors (*see also p.61*). As the plan on page 54 illustrates, putting the garden at an angle can also be combined with changing levels.

THE GARDEN FLOOR

UNLESS YOU ARE DELIBERATELY AIMING to create a dramatic effect, the "flooring" or hard-landscaped areas should be as simple as possible, with the number of different materials kept to a minimum and the finish and colour subtle so that it acts as a perfect foil to surrounding plants. Grass, the traditional surface, does this naturally, and may be necessary for children's play, but in a really small space it often does not repay the work it creates.

PAVING THE WAY

There are so many different materials available today, in so many shapes, textures and colours, that the choice can be quite bewildering. An excellent starting point is the house itself. If built of brick, you may wish to create a unifying link by using the same brick for paths and patio. Check first that it is thoroughly frostproof; you may instead have to pick a matching brick designed for the job. Brick is versatile and can be laid in all sorts of patterns to create different effects. Stretcher bond can be used to make a garden seem wider (*see p.32*). Herringbone pattern (*see p.66*) has a sense of movement, but a square-looking pattern such as basket-weave has a static quality making it ideal for a patio.

Traditionally brick and stone paving have been used in combination, especially with period houses, as both age well together (though stone can be slippery when wet). Imitation paving stones are a fraction of the cost. Some can be rather garish, but

Install power conduits for lighting or water features before laying paving

there are also some excellent reproductions which, once the patina of age has developed, are hard to tell from the real thing. Pre-cast paving slabs need to be selected with care. Avoid over-rough slabs

FLUID GRAVEL
Gravel blends with other materials and with foliage. It is inclined to travel, so keep the surface a little lower than its surround.

RANDOM STONE
The simple textures and soft colours of stone and wood complement one another and provide a perfect foil to surrounding plants.

▲ COBBLED CORNER
*Cobbles add detail
and easily fill in an
awkward corner
around pavers of a
matching colour.*

◄ SETT PIECE
*A single material has
been used throughout
this garden. The
granite setts move
gently through the
space, with the
planting softening the
edges. Small setts are
one of the easiest
hard-surface materials
to lay on an incline.*

in crude colours that clash with plants. Paving levels need to take account of manhole covers and must always be 15cm, or two brick courses, lower than the house damp-proof course. For a professional finish, let the dimensions of the slabs govern the size of a paved area; avoid having to cut them unnecessarily.

CONCRETE PROPOSAL

Most people think concrete harsh and dull but used in a thoughtful way it is possible to create some pleasing finishes. It can be cast to suit all sorts of oddly shaped areas and is reasonably inexpensive. Concrete is made with a mixture of sharp sand and stone or aggregate. If lightly brushed before it sets, you can expose the aggregate and produce an attractive texture. The plan on page 46 uses this finish in panels of brick.

GRAVEL AND TIMBER

Gravel fits smoothly, like a wall-to-wall carpet, into any shape or corner. The surface for a gravel garden (*as on p.45*) has a fairly loose finish. A path, on the other hand, must be firm to the tread. It needs a retaining edge and the gravel should be thinly laid, about 12–18mm deep, over a well-compacted base, then rolled or lightly raked. The crunch of gravel underfoot acts as a deterrent to burglars but it clings to shoes and should not be laid right up to the house door (*see p.40*). Stones of about 10–14mm are a good size.

Decking, made from pressure-treated wood, is useful, especially in dryish climates and to create raised levels (*see p.68*). Joists or supports must be protected from damp soil; the ground beneath should be cleared of topsoil and covered with coarse gravel.

EXPLOITING CHANGES OF LEVEL

WHICHEVER WAY YOUR GARDEN SLOPES, any change of level is worth exploiting for the interest it will add to the overall design (*see pp.34 and 42*). In a small garden, it is worth creating at least one raised area for the benefits it will bring in displaying plants. The changes do not have to be dramatic; small alterations in height can act as a subtle way of separating parts of the garden, for instance, defining the dining area (*see p.38*).

INITIAL CALCULATIONS

Before deciding how to make the most of existing changes of level or whether to create new ones, you need an accurate picture of how much and in what direction the land slopes. Generally, a garden slopes square-on towards or away from the house, but occasionally there is a cross-fall, a diagonal slope. You can do a simple levels survey yourself (*see p.72*), but for more complicated gradients you may need to call on the services of a surveyor. If a large retaining wall (*see p.35*) is needed, because of the weight of soil that will be pressing against it, you may also need to consult a structural engineer. Before opting for a design that needs terracing and therefore a lot of earth moving, consider how easy – or otherwise – access will be for machinery. If it is going to be impossible, work out how much time and effort would be involved in doing it all by hand.

SAFE STEPS
Stable pavers, deeply etched with a criss-cross pattern, are hard-wearing and give a firm foothold. Because this kind of engineering brick is not porous, the steps will not get covered in lichen or moss – a particular problem for steps in shade.

▲WHICH WAY TO TURN
A steep flight of steps in a confined space can look oppressive. Given a mid-way landing with a right-angled turn, the steps become an attractive feature.

◄NEW HEIGHTS
Building tiers of decking is one of the easiest ways of artificially raising height; the planks themselves create a strong sense of direction.

WELL-DESIGNED STEPS

If your design includes steps, there are three important dimensions you need to take into account. The "rise" is the height of each step; the "tread" is the step's depth, the place where you rest your foot; and the "going" is the distance from the first to the last rise (the total of all the treads or the

---

Arrange some lighting by steps that are regularly used at night

---

space required to accommodate the complete flight). In a house, steps tend to be a standard size with quite a steep rise, but this would look out of place in the garden, where you can afford to be more generous. A good comfortable rise is 15cm; you can get an idea of the number of steps you require by dividing this number into

the overall change in level. Don't make steps too shallow, less than 7.5cm say, or they can cause people to trip. A good average depth of tread is 45cm or more – the greater the better. It is important that within the same flight of steps all the rises and treads are exactly the same. Any breaks in their rhythm can make people stumble (*see p.43*).

Steps can be built of any suitable material – brick, stone or timber. In shady areas, do not allow them to develop a slippery surface. Timber steps may need a strip of chicken wire tacked onto the treads.

Wooden decking (*see p.69*) is one of the simplest ways of creating artificial changes of level on flat sites. It is also another, often simpler, way of creating a terrace on a sloping site, using joists fixed to posts of appropriate height to build a flat platform. Where decking is to accommodate heavy furniture, use a construction method that is strong enough to bear the weight.

MAKING A VIRTUE OF NECESSITY

THERE IS ALWAYS A DANGER, when you start to design your garden, that you get carried away with all the exciting parts and forget the mundane details such as storage – where to put the mower and the bikes, where to keep the dustbin so that access is easy but it doesn't look an eyesore, and where to put the "whirly" clothes line. It is important to add these things into the plan at the start so that they can actually add something to the overall design.

CREATIVE STORAGE

Most people don't have a suitable space in the house to store toys, bikes, barbecues, mowers and other garden equipment, so a garden shed is essential. With luck, it can be hidden in a corner, behind tall plants or a purpose-built screen. As with boundary fencing, the shed can be stained or painted a dark shade so that it blends into the background (see p.65), or camouflaged by luxuriant climbing plants. And it won't be quite so obvious if you position it with its door, rather than its longest side, facing the house. But if you simply cannot disguise it, turn it into a feature instead. Give it a distinctive coat of colour, an arch to frame its door, or create an illusory window with a deft piece of trompe l'oeil.

Where there is easy access from the street, you may need to consider a secure lock for your shed. If you don't need to store anything too bulky you might be able to build sufficient storage space into seating (see pp.38 and 50). It is also possible to

> A cleverly designed sandpit can include storage space for toys

buy ready-made benches with hinged seats and storage space. Built-in barbecues should be given cupboards for cooking equipment and fuel, and storage places for toys can be incorporated into play areas.

DIAMONDS OF IVY
An ugly garage wall that forms one side of a shady passage can be concealed behind a lattice of ivy trained along bamboo canes. Pyracantha, too, can be pruned and trained to create a lattice-work of squares.

◄ WORK OF ART
*Almost disappearing
beneath its flowery
canopy of* Clematis
montana, *this
delightful shed, with
its* trompe l'oeil *door,
promises all manner
of delights within.*

▼ DISTANT VIEW
*Instead of hiding the
shed away, this one
has been painted
bright yellow and
turned into a focal
point at the end of a
vista, framed by an
arch – a good
solution for a long,
thin garden.*

WASH-DAY AND DUSTBINS

Many people want to dry their washing
outside, in fresh air. A clothes line stretched
across the garden takes up a lot of room,
but the circular "whirly" type is much
easier to accommodate. However, you will
still need to give it sufficient space for
sheets to flap out in the wind without
catching on nearby plants, or having the
plants stain the washing.

Dustbins are a perennial problem
because they usually have to be sited close
to both the house and front access. A
simple screen of trellis or timber slats, with
climbers weaving through, is the simplest
way of camouflaging the bin, or you could
customize it with spray paints and give it
your own inimitable design. But make sure
the bin men can still recognize it.

PLANS FOR SMALL GARDENS

A SELECTION OF WORKING DESIGNS

THE DESIGN YOU CHOOSE needs to suit the way you want to use your garden and, of course, the site itself. The 20 plans that follow all illustrate different ways of making the most of a small space, as well as suiting a range of lifestyles. Many are low maintenance – a demand usually near the top of most people's lists of priorities – several will increase your sense of privacy (for example, *p.36*) and some use techniques to make the space seem larger (*pp.40 and 54*). Styles vary from formal (*p.66*) to informal (*p.44*) and decidedly modern (*p.70*). The designs also feature all the hard landscaping materials you are likely to want to use from decking (*p.68*) and textured concrete (*p.46*) to paving in brick and stone (*pp.32, 38 and 58*). Gravel is the surface chosen for the designs on pages 40, 44 and 50, and grass for those on 42, 56 and 64. Several combine materials. Grass is generally used if children need space for ball games, but the plan on page 52 shows a good way of incorporating a separate play area. And if entertaining is one of your pleasures, the garden on page 54 would be the place to invite friends for an *al fresco* dinner party.

A LIGHTER TOUCH
Multi-stemmed trees give an airy feel to a small garden. You can achieve the effect by planting young trees in the same hole and letting them grow together, but use only trees that would grow naturally in this way, such as silver birch (Betula pendula) *and alders (for instance,* Alnus cordata *or* A. incana*).*

◄ CREATIVE HEIGHTS *Planting on different levels and in containers can create tiers of colour.*

DIVIDING A LONG, THIN GARDEN

T HE VAST MAJORITY of gardens tend to be long and narrow, but all too often
the moment you walk in your eye is drawn straight to the back fence,
foreshortening the length and making the garden appear smaller than it really
is. By introducing simple divisions, you can break the long view and create an
illusion of greater space and a sense of mystery. The divisions do not block off
complete areas, but give an enticing glimpse of what lies beyond. In this plan,
two short rows of metal poles (of the kind used for scaffolding) extend from
either side towards the centre, forming simple but effective screens.

DESIGN BRIEF

• Shape of garden to
be disguised, so that
it is not so obviously
a long, narrow
rectangle.

• Paving rather than
lawn to keep
maintenance to a
minimum.

• Lots of plants to
soften the boundaries
and hard edges of the
paving, and to create
a sense of privacy.

• Storage space for
garden tools and
family bikes.

Silver birch
(*Betula pendula*)
has been
retained

Small garden
shed for general
storage. Paved
path leads to
shed door

Bench seat in the
quietest, most
secluded area of
the garden

A line of painted tubular
metal poles is used to
create a dividing screen.
They can be wired
together to support
climbers. A matching
line of poles creates a
screen on the other side

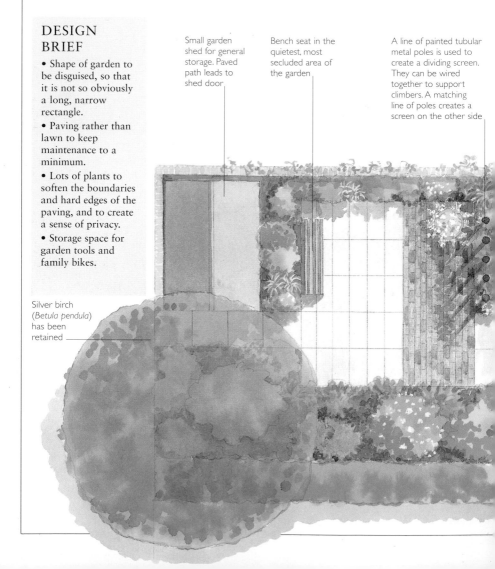

USING SCREENS TO CREATE DIVISION

There are many ways of creating screens to divide a garden. If a border of plants runs around the boundary, the simplest way is to extend this in from each side to form alternate "fingers" of greenery. These can be supplemented by trellis panels, to support climbers, or metal or timber poles – round or square-sawn – that can be painted or stained in a harmonious colour. They need to be set in concrete or into metal fence-post sockets, below ground level, rammed securely into hardcore.

◄ SIMPLE SOLUTION
Trellis makes a good screen that also provides a backdrop for plants without creating shade.

► TREE SCREEN
An exciting feature is created by a screen cut from a piece of weatherproofed blockboard.

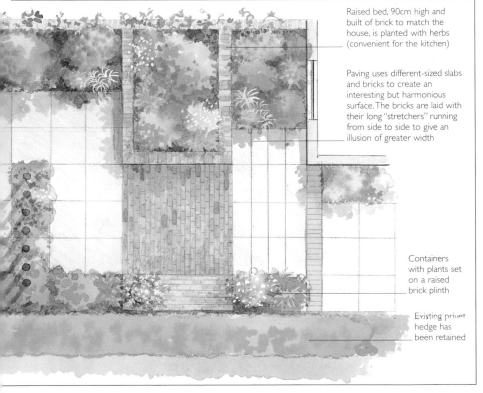

Raised bed, 90cm high and built of brick to match the house, is planted with herbs (convenient for the kitchen)

Paving uses different-sized slabs and bricks to create an interesting but harmonious surface. The bricks are laid with their long "stretchers" running from side to side to give an illusion of greater width

Containers with plants set on a raised brick plinth

Existing privet hedge has been retained

A DOWNHILL SLOPE

USUALLY A CHANGE IN LEVEL within a garden is an advantage and should be exploited to add interest. When the land slopes away from the back of the house, it sometimes feels as though it is "falling away". It helps to lift the area closest to the house to create a level sitting-out terrace, with a broad flight of steps, incorporated into the retaining wall, leading down to the lower level.

Sundial with gravel and brick surround on centre line of steps and house French windows

Whitebeam (Sorbus aria), one of a pair that reinforce the symmetry of the design and frame the view behind

Symmetrical curved lawn on centre line of steps and French windows

Matching raised beds either side of steps

Steps leading down to lawn are paved with same slabs as used for terrace and have 15cm risers

Terrace paved with 45cm square, butt-jointed slabs

DESIGN BRIEF

• Garden to have two flat, level areas, with retaining wall and steps.

• Area for sitting out immediately outside French windows.

• Lawn in lower part of the garden.

• Symmetrical design to include a sundial.

• Luxuriant planting to give a sense of enclosure and to camouflage the boundaries.

_____ Mixed planting "wrapped" around lawn to hide the boundary fence

_____ Retaining wall, 60cm high and built of the same brick as the house, turns the corner and runs along the boundary so that soil does not come into contact with the boundary fence

RETAINING WALLS

Where a garden has a change of level, it is often necessary to provide a retaining wall to hold back the soil at the upper level. Its design and construction are extremely important, as considerable pressure will be exerted by the mass of soil behind it and the water that it contains. If you need a long retaining wall and it is to be more than 1.5m high, you will need to consult a structural engineer. The wall should be thicker at its base and built on strong foundations. Retaining walls are often constructed from concrete blocks and finished with a facing of stone or brick. If built across a garden, a wall must not end abruptly at the boundary fence. Run it along the boundary (see plan opposite) so that soil is not piled against the fence, making it rot. In the right setting, old railway sleepers make simple but attractive retaining walls.

▶ ELEGANT STONE
A traditional wall has been finished with local stone. The band of bricks at its base provides a mowing edge.

▼ WALLS OF WOOD
When laid flat, reclaimed railway sleepers are a quick and easy way of building a series of sturdy low walls.

CONCEALING THE BOUNDARIES

YOU CAN OFTEN MAKE your garden seem larger by concealing the perimeter with luxuriant planting. This can sometimes blend in with neighbouring trees and shrubs so that the garden appears to extend beyond its actual limits, or it can be used to block out unwanted sights entirely. Clothe fencing with a selection of climbers, and "wrap" a mixture of evergreen and deciduous shrubs around the central area. Two interlocking circular lawns make an ideal shape.

DESIGN BRIEF

• Paving next to house to be used for a dining area with easy access to kitchen and sitting room.

• Small, easily maintained area of lawn.

• Ugly boundary fencing to be concealed.

• Planting to give sense of privacy, retaining existing tree.

• A quiet and relaxing place to sit.

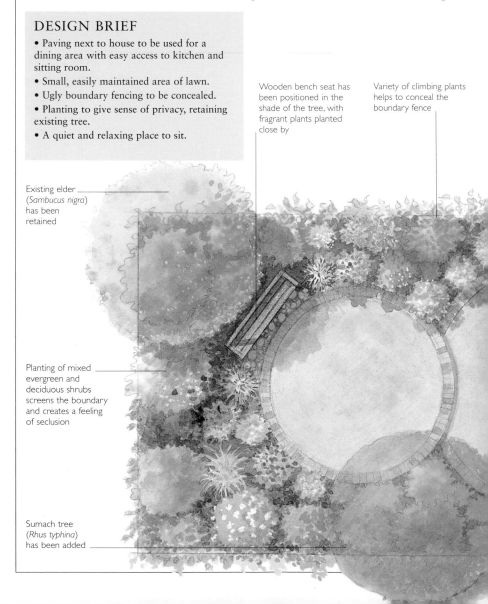

Wooden bench seat has been positioned in the shade of the tree, with fragrant plants planted close by

Variety of climbing plants helps to conceal the boundary fence

Existing elder (*Sambucus nigra*) has been retained

Planting of mixed evergreen and deciduous shrubs screens the boundary and creates a feeling of seclusion

Sumach tree (*Rhus typhina*) has been added

PLANTS FOR SCREENING

Make a wide perimeter border with room enough for plenty of plants to obscure the boundary. Grade the shrubs by height, with the smallest at the front. Choose plants carefully so that you create attractive combinations of foliage colour and texture. Bamboos and grasses are a good choice, as well as bold-leaved shrubs such as fatsia. There are plenty of flowering climbers, such as clematis and honeysuckle, to provide colour and scent.

VIBURNUM RHYTIDOPHYLLUM
A vigorous evergreen shrub; berries follow the flowers.

YUSHANIA ANCEPS
Bamboos help create a sound barrier. This evergreen grows to 4m but can be invasive.

ACTINIDIA KOLOMIKTA
Striking climber for sheltered walls. Plants need time to achieve their finest colour.

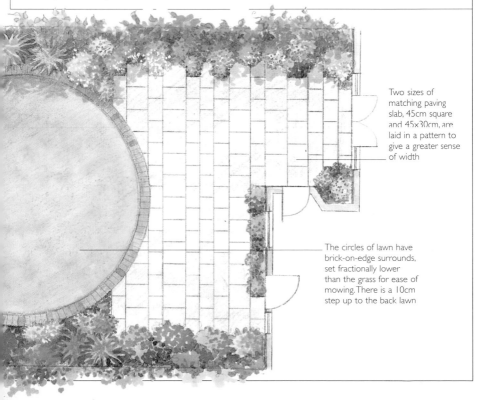

Two sizes of matching paving slab, 45cm square and 45×30cm, are laid in a pattern to give a greater sense of width

The circles of lawn have brick-on-edge surrounds, set fractionally lower than the grass for ease of mowing. There is a 10cm step up to the back lawn

CHANGING LEVELS

IT IS EASY, even in a flat garden, to introduce some simple changes in level by creating a number of steps within the design. Here, the first two steps extend all the way across the garden, to maximize the sense of width; the last step, somewhat narrower, leads up to the barbecue and dining area. Bricks laid on edge provide a comfortable 10cm rise – all the steps in this garden have been built in this way, creating a rhythm that will not cause people to stumble (*see p.27*). The topsoil that is removed in order to lay the paving (which must be laid on subsoil and hardcore) can be used to fill the raised bed (*see p.17*).

Dining area with built-in benches that have hinged seats with storage beneath

Built-in barbecue with tiled surround and storage space

Mixed planting of perennials and shrubs includes several with strong, architectural form and foliage

Bricks laid in "running bond" pattern – with their stretchers across the garden – help to emphasize width

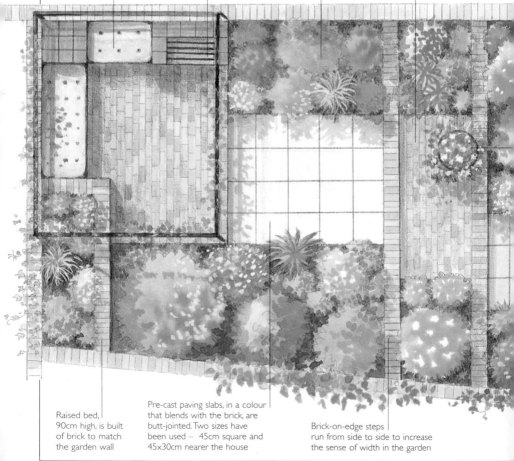

Raised bed, 90cm high, is built of brick to match the garden wall

Pre-cast paving slabs, in a colour that blends with the brick, are butt-jointed. Two sizes have been used – 45cm square and 45x30cm nearer the house

Brick-on-edge steps run from side to side to increase the sense of width in the garden

DESIGN BRIEF

- Built-in barbecue and dining area, with storage.
- Paved surface to harmonize with house.
- Minimum maintenance.
- Changes of level to be added to give extra interest. Boring shape to be disguised.
- Mixture of shrubs, perennials and climbers to soften walls and paving.
- Somewhere to put containers.

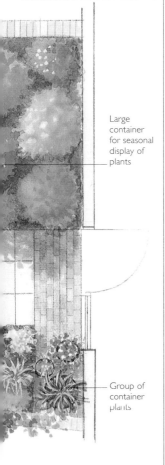

Large container for seasonal display of plants

Group of container plants

PATTERNS IN PAVING

Paving tends to come in two forms: natural, cut stone, usually laid in a random pattern, and manufactured pre-cast slabs, bricks and pavers, which can be laid to create a whole variety of patterns (*see p.24*). The size of the slabs, or the pattern or "grid" that you create, should dictate the dimensions of paved areas. Avoid odd-sized areas of hard landscaping that result in cutting awkward shapes in the paving materials. For the most part, the hard landscape should be low key, providing a perfect foil to the planting, but patterns can be extremely useful in deceiving the eye and making a garden seem wider or longer, or for creating a unifying effect.

◀ON THE LINE
A mixture of old railway sleepers and granite setts creates a simple but pleasing pattern. The bold lines it creates could be used to make a garden seem wider or longer.

▼ GRID LOCK
A fairly dominant grid pattern of brick with panels of paving slabs changes initial perception of the shape of this garden. The pattern determines the size and shape of the planting areas.

FOCUS OF ATTENTION

H ERE, THE DESIGN HAS BEEN SET at an angle of 45° to the house, along the diagonal. Because this is the longest line, it creates the illusion of greater space (*see pp.23, 54 and 68*). One of the drawbacks of gravel is the way it clings to the soles of shoes (especially trainers). The paved area by the door into the house gives a chance for chippings to fall off. The central focal point has a unifying effect and adds interest to the garden all year.

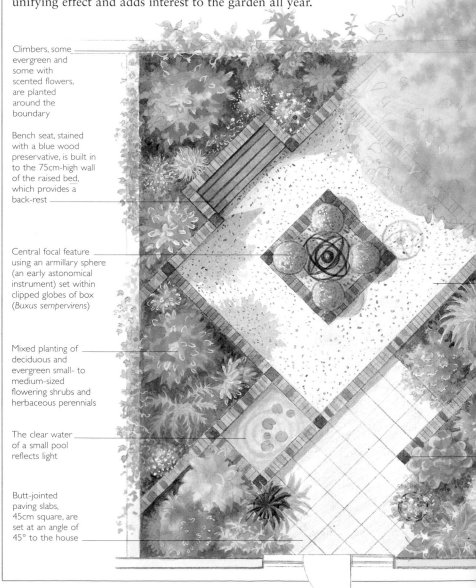

Climbers, some evergreen and some with scented flowers, are planted around the boundary

Bench seat, stained with a blue wood preservative, is built in to the 75cm-high wall of the raised bed, which provides a back-rest

Central focal feature using an armillary sphere (an early astonomical instrument) set within clipped globes of box (*Buxus sempervirens*)

Mixed planting of deciduous and evergreen small- to medium-sized flowering shrubs and herbaceous perennials

The clear water of a small pool reflects light

Butt-jointed paving slabs, 45cm square, are set at an angle of 45° to the house

DESIGN BRIEF

• Garden to be made to look as large as possible.
• Fairly formal look with year-round interest. Low maintenance.
• Tree to create some shade and hide view.
• Introduction of a little colour in materials.
• Small pool.
• Somewhere to sit.
• Inclusion of a garden ornament (armillary sphere), a family heirloom.

USING FOCAL POINTS

Focal points are used to draw the eye in a certain direction or simply to create extra interest throughout the garden. They can either take the form of statues or pieces of sculpture, including sundials, birdbaths and ceramic pots or urns, or you can use handsome plants with striking foliage or colour. Place focal points at the centre of a space or at the ends of long vistas; sometimes they can usefully link two sections (*see p.34*). Or they can be subtly positioned within an area of planting, to create an element of surprise.

◄ FOLIAGE FOCUS
Bold foliage stands out well against surrounding greenery. Spear-shaped leaves, such as those of phormiums and yuccas, create the right kind of impact; the container, too, needs to be worthy of a prominent place.

▼ IN THE FRAME
The criss-cross backdrop of a woven arbour enhances the effectiveness as a focal point of this classic-style sundial.

Paulownia tomentosa (foxglove tree)

Central area of gravel (see *p.45* for *method of laying*). Its finished level is slightly lower than the bordering bands of brick, so that it does not spill onto paving or into the pond

Brick-on-edge step, 10cm high. Bands of brick have frostproof cobalt blue glazed blocks at junctions and corners

DEALING WITH AN UPHILL SLOPE

A GARDEN WITH AN UPHILL SLOPE tends visually to come towards you, especially near the house, making the overall space seem smaller. You can lessen this effect by creating two separate levels linked by a flight of steps (*see also the downhill garden, p.34*). In this design, the upper lawn is divided from the lower lawn by raised beds built from old railway sleepers. An overhead pergola extends from side to side, giving a sense of extra width; it is echoed by the pergola that frames the entrance to the garden from the side passage.

A pair of whitebeams (*Sorbus aria* 'Lutescens') with attractive grey-green foliage hide neighbouring houses and suit the symmetrical design

Pergola (built from pressure-treated square-sawn timber, see p.49) is stained blue to match the one over the side passage. The pergola acts as both a screen and a "doorway" into the upper lawn, and supports climbing plants

Retaining walls and central flight of steps are built from old railway sleepers

Upper lawn with mowing edge of brick

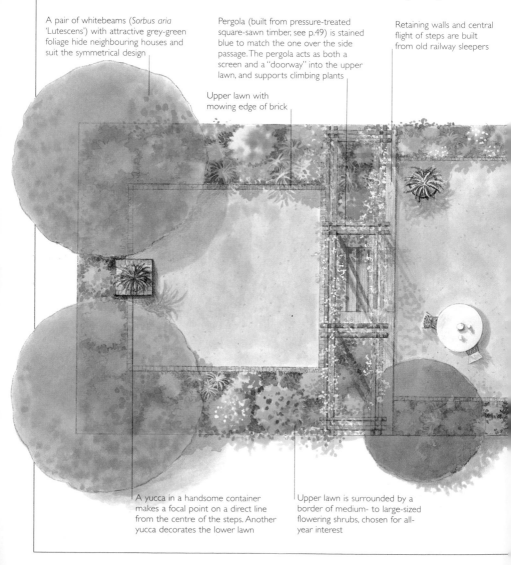

A yucca in a handsome container makes a focal point on a direct line from the centre of the steps. Another yucca decorates the lower lawn

Upper lawn is surrounded by a border of medium- to large-sized flowering shrubs, chosen for all-year interest

DESIGN BRIEF

- Garden to have two flat areas of lawn.
- Pergola with climbers to be used to divide the garden.
- Medium-sized trees to be planted at rear to hide houses beyond.
- Lightly shaded area for two to sit and eat outside.
- Planting to provide all-year interest.

CREATING STEPS

When well-designed, steps need not be purely functional but can become an important garden feature. Bricks and slabs are the most commonly used materials, to match other paved areas, but railway sleepers (*below*) are particularly suitable for some garden styles and are quick and easy to install. Steps must have uniform "rises" (*see p.27*), and on a long flight, try to include regular landings. Where they form part of a pathway they should be the same width as the path. If set into a retaining wall, measurements and materials need to be planned at the same time. Step edges are made more visible – and safer – if the treads slightly overhang the risers. Where steps are used regularly after dark, they need to be lit (*see p.55*); when done well this only enhances their value as a feature.

Lower lawn has a brick surround; this is set slightly lower than the grass for easy mowing and eliminates the task of edging

Plant-filled containers decorate the side passage

Brick paving leads through to the garden under a blue-stained wooden pergola

◄ STEP UP
A simple pair of steps has been built into a brick wall, using matching bricks.

▼ EASY FLIGHT
Railway sleepers, laid flat and infilled with hardcore and gravel, make one of the simplest ways to build a flight of steps with a slight curve.

An Informal Gravel Garden

Gravel makes the ideal surface if you want to create an informal feel to the garden, since the plants can grow through it and give a soft, blurred edge to the planting. A pergola makes a "doorway" leading from the paved area into the gravel sitting area, with a seat in the shade of a small flowering cherry. The sound of water is provided by a millstone bubble fountain, set among graded pebbles to blend in with the gravel.

Bench seat and timber pergola, both stained to match the pergola near the house, benefit from the light shade of a flowering cherry tree

The colour of the gravel blends with the paving and house; 10–14mm pea gravel is an ideal size for areas like this

DESIGN BRIEF

- Informal style with gravel.
- A feeling of privacy and screening from neighbours (design to take account of existing tree at rear).
- Small water feature, with sound of water.
- Interesting, architectural planting for a keen gardener.
- York stone paving immediately outside house.
- Outdoor dining table and chairs.
- Somewhere to sit in dappled shade.
- Pergolas with climbers.
- Some containers with plants near house.

Silver birch (*Betula pendula*) in a neighbour's garden

Bubble fountain with pebble surround

Mixed planting encloses the informal gravel area

Stained timber pergola (see p.49) links the paved and gravel areas

Random York stone paving leads into the house, separating gravel area from doorway (see p.40)

GOOD PLANTS FOR GRAVEL

Plants with strong shape and colour are set off to perfection in gravel. However, because it is an ideal growing medium for self-sown seedlings, including weeds, you must decide which areas you want to keep free of plants. Remove the topsoil in that area down to a firm subsoil base and then, if necessary, add a layer of clean hardcore, sufficiently deep for a 30–60mm layer of gravel to be laid on top to bring the area back up to ground level. For greater weed discouragement, before laying the gravel you can cover the area with geotextile or black plastic. If you then want to make planting pockets, simply dig out planting holes and fill with good topsoil. Spread a gravel mulch around the plants to blend with their surround.

BOLD STATEMENT
Phormiums look particularly good with gravel around their simple, bold leaves, which can be green, purple or variegated.

GHOST IN THE GARDEN
Eryngium giganteum *(known as Miss Willmott's ghost) has a luminous quality at dusk. It is biennial but self-seeds.*

GREEN EDGING
The frothy green flowers of Alchemilla conjuncta (above), or A. mollis, spill prettily over gravel giving a soft edge.

DRAMATIC FORM
Agaves are handsome but not fully hardy. In cold areas, "plunge" in a pot; in winter, lift and protect under glass.

GEOMETRIC APPEAL

PEOPLE WHO LEAD busy lives usually want a garden that requires little regular maintenance. Quite often that means no lawn. Here, a strong geometric pattern of brick bands infilled with panels of exposed aggregate provides an area for entertaining and relaxing. The exposed aggregate gives an interesting texture, with subtle touches of colour added by the brick. The surface doesn't get slippery when wet, and the only attention needed is the occasional sweep.

DESIGN BRIEF

• Low maintenance and no lawn. Easy-to-care-for planting, with a mixture of flowering shrubs for year-round interest.

• A summerhouse, plus additional space for seating when entertaining and relaxing.

• Space for an old sundial inherited from a relative's much admired garden.

• Sound of water from a small water feature.

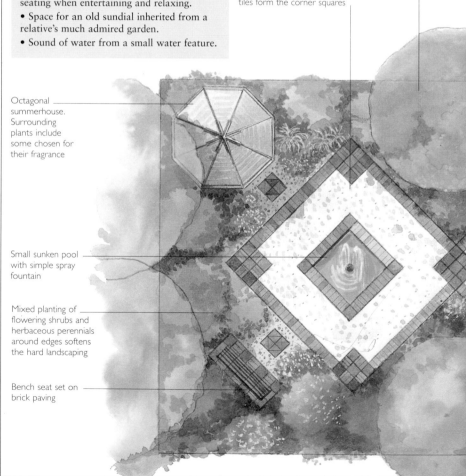

Garden floor pattern formed by bands of blue-grey engineering bricks, laid on edge, infilled with exposed aggregate. Matching colour tiles form the corner squares

Pair of flowering cherries, *Prunus* 'Taihaku', emphasize the symmetry of the design

Octagonal summerhouse. Surrounding plants include some chosen for their fragrance

Small sunken pool with simple spray fountain

Mixed planting of flowering shrubs and herbaceous perennials around edges softens the hard landscaping

Bench seat set on brick paving

USING EXPOSED AGGREGATE

Although concrete has a poor image with many people, it is a very versatile, relatively inexpensive material and looks especially good if you expose the aggregate – the stones within the mix. The colour and texture will vary according to the type and size of the stones selected. To expose the aggregate, lightly brush the surface while the concrete is still "green" – when it has a greenish hue just prior to setting hard. Concrete is laid *in situ*, and needs to be contained within an edging of wood, brick or paving slabs, which can be decorative, as in the plan below.

▶ MAKING THE GRADE
Different size aggregates
create a coarse
or fine texture.
For the
aggregate,
choose a stone
that blends with
its surroundings.

▲ CONTRASTING TEXTURES
A "fluid" material, concrete
can be laid in unusual shapes,
broken by bands of brick.

A series of diamond shapes makes an unusual pathway from house into garden

Wooden bench is paired by a sundial on the opposite side of the garden

A TRIANGULAR PLOT

YOU MAY BE FACED with an irregular or
particularly awkward shape but, in a small
area, you will still want to create the illusion of
greater space. In this long triangular garden, the
pathway leads the eye from one side to the
other, and a pergola placed midway, at an
angle to the house, helps to break up the
length into two separate areas. Don't
neglect a difficult far corner, such as this
garden has, letting the space go to
waste. It can make a good place to
hide the shed.

Mixed planting of medium
and large shrubs, deciduous
and evergreen, in a fairly
deep border, helps to hide
boundary fencing

Sunken sandpit (with cover)
is in full view of house so
that a watchful eye can be
kept on the children. Six
paving slabs have been
retained for filling in when it
is no longer needed

Existing small
tree on
boundary has
been retained

DESIGN BRIEF

- Paved play area near the house, with a small sunken sandpit.
- As large a lawn as possible.
- Plenty of plants around the perimeter to mask the boundaries.
- Some small- to medium-sized trees.
- Pergola for climbing roses and honeysuckle.
- Small, unobtrusive shed for storage.

— Medium-sized tree and pergola help to break up the length of the garden while, at the same time, the pergola links the two areas of lawn. The path leads to a seat under a tree and shed tucked away in the far corner

— Raised bed, 45cm high, built of brick

— Mixture of paving slabs and bricks used to create paths and patio

— Deep border backed by tall shrubs, many of them evergreen, helps to create privacy from neighbouring house

A PLACE FOR PERGOLAS

Pergolas can play an important role within a design. They not only provide a framework for climbing plants but can also make a "doorway" leading from one area to another. They can frame a focal point or distant view, or, as in the garden left (*and plan on p.42*), create a visual division between two areas. Make them at least 2.25m tall, higher if they are to support climbers, and over 2.5m if the plants have hanging flowers, such as wisteria. The longer and more abundantly festooned with plants a pergola is, the stronger it needs to be, as it will be vulnerable to prevailing winds.

▲ NATURAL WOOD
If a pergola is to be covered in climbers, make it as durable as possible. Use pressure-treated timber and give it extra coats of preservative, perhaps in an interesting shade.

◀ METAL APPEAL
Metal gives a lighter look to a pergola. Whatever material you choose, the structure must always be securely anchored, and capable of taking the weight of the climbing plants you choose when they are fully grown

SHADE AND RELAXATION

AREAS OF DAPPLED SHADE make pleasant places to sit and relax, especially in a city in summer, and are definitely preferable if you like to eat outside. Even in urban environments, it is possible to evoke a woodland feel with lots of cool greenery. Trees such as amelanchier, golden-leaved *Robinia pseudoacacia* 'Frisia' and cherries like *Prunus sargentii* cast the right sort of shade. Some hinged bench seating under one of them (*see below*) will provide useful storage space.

Tree in neighbouring garden

Shade-loving plants create an informal feel and disguise the gravel's edge

Gravel is laid over geotextile (see p.45) to prevent weeds and self-seedlings from taking firm root

Purpose-designed tree seat (under existing tree). The top of the seat lifts to provide storage space

Simple millstone fountain with naturalistic surround of cobbles and smaller shingle

DESIGN BRIEF

- Paved area adjacent to the house.
- An informal area of gravel, enclosed by favourite plants, including ferns, bamboos, spiraeas, hydrangeas, hellebores and hostas.
- Seat under the tree in the centre of the garden.
- Somewhere to store gardening tools.
- A secluded place to sit and read.

—— Group of three silver birch trees (*Betula pendula*)

—— Woven willow arbour

—— Two brick-on-edge steps lead up to the gravel area. The gravel's surface is slightly lower than the top of the brick to prevent the chippings spilling over

—— Short lateral bands of brick run through the random pattern of the York stone paving, helping to create a sense of width

SECLUDED ARBOURS

Arbours are traditionally quiet places of retreat. In the great classic gardens they were often made in rustic style, with gnarled branches and elaborate decoration. Today they are likely to be much more modest, perhaps purchased in kit form from a catalogue. Choose materials to suit the style of your garden – wirework, wood or even living willow (*see below*). It is quite simple to construct your own design from ready-treated timber and trellis panels; paint or stain it in a suitable colour, if you wish. If you train scented climbers over and around, you will be able to catch their fragrance while you sit. Arbours are best sited on the edge of a well planted area, in light shade. Position them so that they either give a general view of the garden or, if you can offer a glimpse of fine countryside, let them look towards the landscape beyond.

▲ RURAL RETREAT
A seat with its own canopy woven from hazel and willow lends a romantic, rural air, set against a leafy planting of trees and shrubs.

◀ GREEN HIDEAWAY
A living willow arbour will need very regular training and trimming but makes an interesting project for an enthusiast. Specialist willow suppliers will advise on varieties to plant.

A FAMILY GARDEN

As CHILDREN GET OLDER, they will want a reasonable-sized lawn for ball games and, if space allows, an adventure play area that they feel is theirs, away from the adults (here, it is separated by low palisade fencing). Often it helps to screen the play area from neighbours with some small to medium trees, so they don't feel they are being spied on from climbing frames or play towers. Safety must have priority (*see right*). A shed will be essential for storing bikes, toys, garden furniture and tools, and may have to double as a workshop.

DESIGN BRIEF

- Large lawn for ball games surrounded by tough shrubs.
- An adventure play area with safe surface.
- Sitting area under existing walnut tree.
- Large garden shed, with easy access, to use as a workshop and for storage.
- A built-in barbecue for family entertainment.
- Small herb garden and some raised beds.

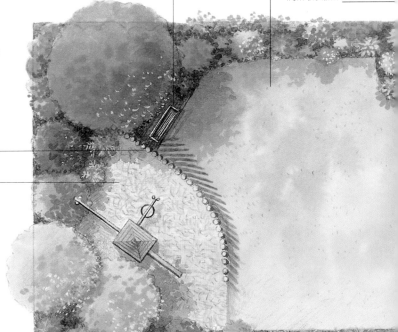

Lawn provides children with space for ball games. It has been created by sowing a specially selected "hard-wearing" seed mix

Garden seat under walnut tree

Existing tree has been retained and some tough shrubs planted to screen barbecue area and shed from the lawn

Wooden palisade fencing, gradually descending in height towards the play area entrance, stops bark from spilling onto the lawn and defines children's area

Adventure play area, with climbing frame, swing and slide, has a thick covering of play-bark on the ground to prevent injury

Medium-size trees act as a screen between play area and neighbouring gardens

CREATING PLAY AREAS

A play area must be designed with safety as the major consideration (*see p.15*). Make sure equipment, whether bought or home-made, is securely installed. Swings and similar items need sufficient space around and regular checks for wear and tear. Deep sand (use washed sand) or play-bark provides a safe landing. Equipment need not be highly sophisticated but can be the sort that stimulates creative play.

▲ FUN IN THE SAND
Plastic matting makes an extra surface for wheeling toys and can be used to double as a cover to prevent pets from fouling the sand.

◄ SWINGS AND LADDERS
Wooden play equipment (it must be splinter free) blends into a garden setting. Modular plastic kits are bright and easy to assemble.

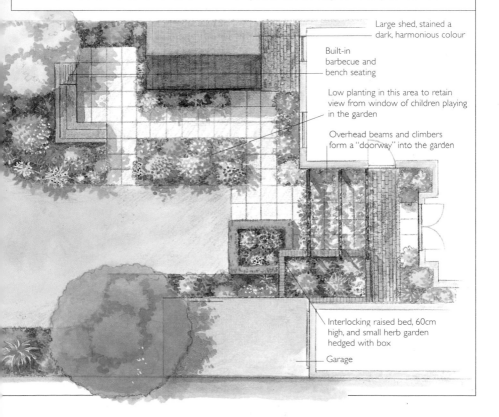

Large shed, stained a dark, harmonious colour

Built-in barbecue and bench seating

Low planting in this area to retain view from window of children playing in the garden

Overhead beams and climbers form a "doorway" into the garden

Interlocking raised bed, 60cm high, and small herb garden hedged with box

Garage

A PLACE FOR ENTERTAINING

MANY PEOPLE want their garden to be an "outdoor room", where they can entertain family and friends. Like the gardens on pages 40 and 68, this is set at an angle of 45° to create maximum space for the barbecue and dining area. There is plenty of room for reclining chairs and other furniture, with the sound of water and lots of lush, leafy plants to create a relaxing atmosphere.

Large-leaved
Paulownia tomentosa
(foxglove tree)
planted to screen
an ugly view from
the dining area

Climbers cover the boundary
walls to increase the sense of
lushness in the planting

Built-in barbecue
with its own storage
cupboards

Groups of purple-
leaved cordylines
(cabbage palms) are
among the striking
foliage plants that
help give the garden
an exotic feel

Bubble fountain,
surrounded by
shingle that blends
with the paving,
provides the sound
of moving water

DESIGN BRIEF

- Barbecue and dining area; table to be lightly shaded in summer.
- Low maintenance.
- Subtle lighting for after-dark entertaining.
- Water features that will provide the sound of moving water and look good when lit up.
- Lush planting using plenty of architectural foliage plants to create an exotic, sub-tropical feel.

LIGHTING UP THE GARDEN

Lighting adds a new dimension – use it for entertaining, and to help with safety and security, by illuminating steps, steep paths and doorways. Low-voltage systems using a transformer give a low light but are good for creating atmosphere in a small space. Stronger lights need mains electricity delivered via armoured conduit laid at least 45cm deep (if a sitting area is next to the house, lights are fairly easily installed on the wall). The range available is enormous, so it is worth consulting specialists on what can be achieved – they will often give a demonstration. Always ask a qualified electrician to install it.

◄ UPWARD BEAM
Lights shining up through plants pick out interesting foliage shapes and colours. They can also be used to highlight statues.

▼ AFTER DUSK
Candlelight creates an intimate ambience for entertaining, while uplighters add drama by illuminating the centre of the garden and its tree.

A semi-circular brick wall encloses the dining area – the table echoes its shape. A structure of overhead beams, lightly covered with climbing plants, casts pleasant shade

Raised pools, 45cm and 30cm high, are connected by a stone slab over which water gently cascades. At 45cm, the sides of the top pool can be used for seating

Levels have been slightly raised to add interest to a flat area, using two brick-on-edge steps

Paving slabs and brick are mixed to create an interesting surface. Their diagonal pattern creates a feeling of space

DIFFERENT WAYS WITH GRASS

I T IS POSSIBLE to create changes of mood within a garden, as you move from one end to the other, by varying the surfaces and styles of planting. Near the house, panels of exposed aggregate (*see p.47*) and brick provide a practical hard surface by the two doors. An irregularly shaped, conventional mown lawn has a much softer feel and makes an area of natural transition to the wilder part at the end, with its meadow-like surround of long grass studded with flowers.

DESIGN BRIEF

- Practical, hard-wearing surface by house.
- Simple lawn, surrounded by mixed planting, retaining flowering cherry tree.
- "Wild" area with trees and secluded seat.
- Garden shed for storage.
- A little shade immediately outside house.

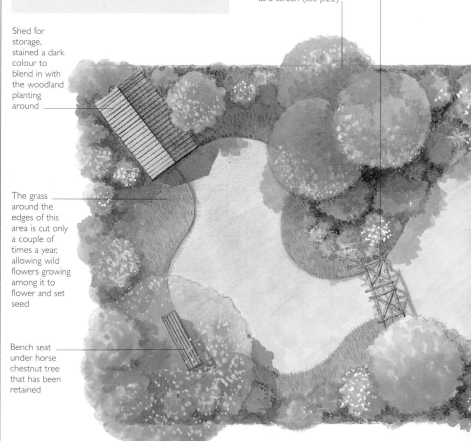

Small trees create seclusion at the end of the garden and privacy from the neighbouring garden. The planting either side of the arch acts as a screen (see p.22)

Rustic arch, with honeysuckle, leads through to a "wild" garden area

Shed for storage, stained a dark colour to blend in with the woodland planting around

The grass around the edges of this area is cut only a couple of times a year, allowing wild flowers growing among it to flower and set seed

Bench seat under horse chestnut tree that has been retained

TRANSFORMING THE LAWN

If you want to get away from the conventional close-cut lawn, try creating patterns in grass by cutting it to different heights. A meadow look is the easiest to achieve. Paths can be cut through areas of long grass (*right*), or a swathe of grass, peppered with wild flowers, can be left uncut around a central, regularly mown area (*as in this plan*). A meadow area would be cut about twice a year, the first time not until the wild flowers have set seed. When developing an existing lawn into meadow, it is best to plant small plants among the grass. If starting from scratch, you can sow a prepared mix of grass and wild-flower seed. Striking effects can be created, too, by cutting grass in maze-like patterns, or making a bull's-eye of alternate long and short rings.

PATHS OF DELIGHT
Use a rotary mower to cut paths through rough grass. The grass will grow again soon enough if you want to change their route.

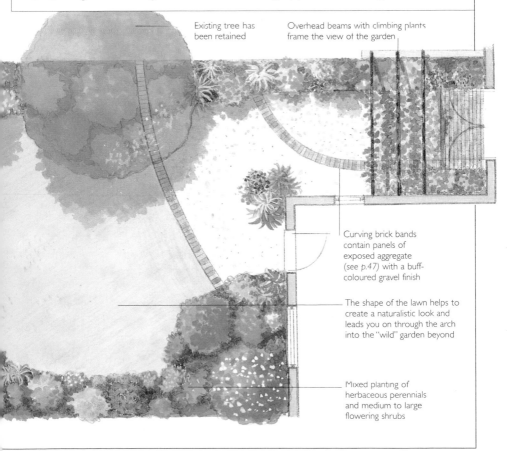

Existing tree has been retained

Overhead beams with climbing plants frame the view of the garden

Curving brick bands contain panels of exposed aggregate (see p.47) with a buff-coloured gravel finish

The shape of the lawn helps to create a naturalistic look and leads you on through the arch into the "wild" garden beyond

Mixed planting of herbaceous perennials and medium to large flowering shrubs

EASY ACCESS, LOW MAINTENANCE

THIS GARDEN HAS BEEN DESIGNED for someone who uses a wheelchair and needs space to manoeuvre, but it would equally suit anybody with bending difficulties. Interest has been created in the paved surfaces by using different sized slabs mixed with areas of brick. A large part of the planting is in raised beds, and there are several seats to choose from for rest and relaxation.

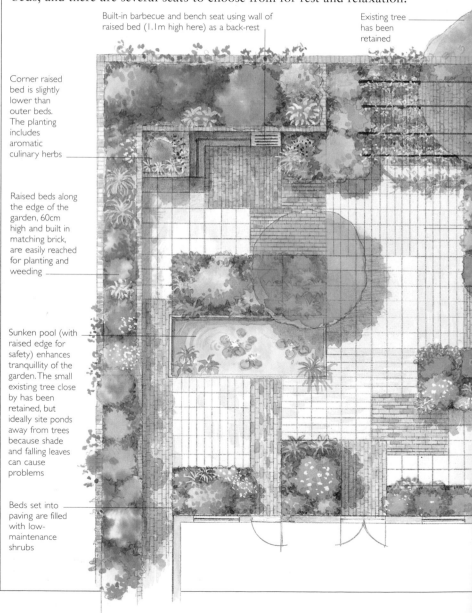

Built-in barbecue and bench seat using wall of raised bed (1.1m high here) as a back-rest

Existing tree has been retained

Corner raised bed is slightly lower than outer beds. The planting includes aromatic culinary herbs

Raised beds along the edge of the garden, 60cm high and built in matching brick, are easily reached for planting and weeding

Sunken pool (with raised edge for safety) enhances tranquillity of the garden. The small existing tree close by has been retained, but ideally site ponds away from trees because shade and falling leaves can cause problems

Beds set into paving are filled with low-maintenance shrubs

DESIGN BRIEF

- Open areas of paving to allow easy movement in a wheelchair. No steps.
- Raised beds with low maintenance planting to include scented foliage and flowers.
- Easily accessible dining and sitting areas in sun and dappled shade.
- Shed for storage.
- Water feature with fish.

Overhead beams and climbers provide a sitting area with dappled shade

Mixture of pre-cast slabs and bricks adds interest to the paving, which is designed for both easy access and easy maintenance

Simple bench seat set into a niche in yew hedge

Large storage shed with wide doors and brick path leading to it for easy access

MAKING RAISED BEDS

These can be built of timber, stone or more often brick. Because of the weight of soil, large beds, higher than eight brick courses, need concrete foundations twice the thickness of the wall. It is essential that drainage is good. Break up the subsoil at the bottom and add a base layer of clean hardcore before filling with good quality topsoil to a depth of 45cm (*see p.17*). Beds are often 90cm high (1.1m if there is a barbecue in front), but wheelchair users will find 60cm a better height. Disabled gardeners may find handles or rails fixed to the wall helpful.

◄ HIGH VALUE
Large sections of timber such as old railway sleepers can be set vertically or laid flat. Stout log roll can be used, if the lower half is set into the ground.

▼ TAKING A TUMBLE
Raised beds ideally suit trailing plants that cascade over the edge. The top of the wall itself needs a smooth finish, of either coping stones or a row of engineering or weatherproof bricks on edge.

THROUGH THE LOOKING GLASS

BY THE CLEVER USE OF MIRRORS you can make even the smallest garden appear larger. In this tiny town courtyard, mirrors have been placed inside two archways to give the impression they lead to other parts of the garden. Without the mirrors, which also reflect light, such dense planting in an enclosed space would create a feeling of claustrophobia. Experiment with the positioning of mirrors to discover the effects that can be achieved (*see also p.68*).

Mirror set in a wrought-iron archway makes it seem as though the garden extends beyond

Border is planted with a mixture of evergreen and deciduous, flowering and foliage shrubs

York stone paving is edged with brick that matches the garden wall

Steps lead down to basement. Retaining walls edge the beds on either side

Steps lead up to house back door

DESIGN BRIEF

• An illusion of greater space.
• Lots of interesting foliage plants, in a border all around the boundary, with climbers clothing the walls.
• Tree in corner of garden to be retained.
• Paved surface that will complement existing cast iron garden furniture and will also be suitable for steps leading up to door.

Medium-sized tree, which casts light shade, has been retained. The planting around it includes bold foliage plants such as bamboos, laurels and ferns

USING MIRRORS

Check any mirror you intend using is suitable for outside; not all can withstand the weather. Other materials can be used instead, for instance a mirror-simulating fabric used for exhibitions and stage sets. You can use frames to conceal the mirror's edges, such as an arch, trellising or an old window frame, or hide them behind foliage. Cunningly placed next to water, mirrors can make a small pool seem twice its size.

◀ON REFLECTION
Mirrors can be used to play tricks or purely as ornament. With its pretty frame, like a mosaic of stained glass, this one adds lightness and brightness among the plants.

▼JUST AN ILLUSION
An arch looks as though it leads through to another part of the garden. In reality, it contains a carefully sited mirror. Avoid placing a mirror near the entrance to a garden. It will fail to deceive if you catch a glimpse of yourself the moment you walk in.

A second mirror is concealed in a wrought-iron archway, again making it look as though the garden extends into an area beyond

Mixed planting under house windows includes several aromatic plants

A TINY COURTYARD

KEEP THE DESIGN SIMPLE and it is surprising how many features can be fitted into a very small space. Here, you walk out onto York stone paving, then take a step down into the central gravelled area. Raised beds, in a brick that matches the house, build symmetry into the design, with a raised pool and wall-mounted water spout providing the gentle sound of falling water. Overhead beams, wired to support climbers, create shade for the dining area on a hot day.

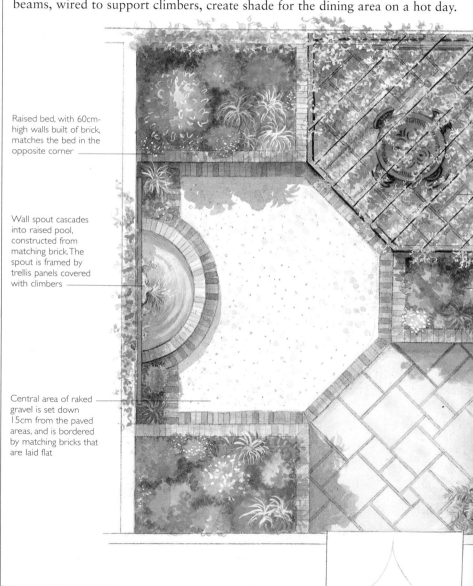

Raised bed, with 60cm-high walls built of brick, matches the bed in the opposite corner

Wall spout cascades into raised pool, constructed from matching brick. The spout is framed by trellis panels covered with climbers

Central area of raked gravel is set down 15cm from the paved areas, and is bordered by matching bricks that are laid flat

DESIGN BRIEF

- Combination of gravel and stone paving for the garden's surface.
- Symmetrical, fairly formal look.
- Low maintenance planting in raised beds.
- Water feature to provide the sound of tumbling water.
- Dining area for four, with overhead shade cast by a canopy of climbers.

Corner panels of trellis support several clematis, chosen to flower in different seasons

Dining area with overhead beams, wired to support a grape vine that casts dappled shade. York stone paves the floor, as in the opposite corner

Raised bed, built of brick and 60cm high – the same height as the two corner beds – is in direct line with the wall spout

York stone paving, laid in a random pattern and set at an angle of 45° to the house

WATER FEATURES

In small gardens, water features are best kept simple, but no matter what size or style you choose (*see p.16*), it is wise to take a specialist supplier's advice on the most suitable liner, pump or fountain to give the results you want. Moving water features generally involve laying electrical conduit and so are best planned in at the outset, before paving is put down, but they extend the range of options to water spouts (*below*) and millstone and cobblestone fountains (*as in the designs on pp.44, 50 and 54*), which have a continuous flow of bubbling water. This type of feature, which does not have a standing reservoir of water, is suitable for gardens with children. Pools in bowls (*below*) also look good set into decking (*see p.68*).

▲ LION'S TASK
A trough of pebbles makes an attractive reservoir for a water spout to trickle into.

◄ ALL IN A BOWL
Use a waterproof half-barrel or cast-iron or glazed ceramic bowl to create a pool that involves no construction work. Since small volumes of water may freeze solid, such pools may need taking inside during winter.

MAKING ROOM FOR VEGETABLES

EVEN IN A SMALL GARDEN, many people want to include a space for growing vegetables without spoiling the overall appearance. Most culinary herbs and some vegetables, for instance lettuces and wigwams of climbing beans, can be incorporated into the general planting; many other crops need a specific area where they can be accompanied by a compost heap and greenhouse. Here, a curving hedge makes an attractive screen that is an intrinsic part of the design.

DESIGN BRIEF

- Area for vegetables with small greenhouse and double compost bin.
- Patio with raised pool and built-in barbecue.
- Herb garden near kitchen door.
- Shed with easy access for bikes, and space for "whirly" clothes-drier and concealed dustbin.
- Mixed planting to include flowering shrubs and retain three trees, with seat under one.

Vegetable garden is largely hidden by the clipped hedge. An existing tree has been retained to shade the seat – a compromise since vegetables grow better without competition from tree roots and in a light, open space

Border of low-growing perennials and shrubs at foot of hedge

Double compost bin, so that material can be added to one side while the other heap is decomposing

Freestanding greenhouse, with brick paths giving easy access to it, the compost heap and the vegetable patch

Clipped hedge with medium to large flowering shrubs behind to conceal the boundary

Existing small tree has been retained

COMBINING FUNCTION AND FEATURE

Most gardens have to accommodate the practical and less attractive needs of everyday life, such as washing line, dustbin and shed. For a satisfactory solution, these should be worked into the overall design at the outset. Dustbins can be hidden by a trellis screen, but storage space will be at a premium. Hinged wooden seats (*see p.50*) are excellent for stowing tools, and built-in barbecues should be given their own cupboard space. With a little flair you can make a feature of the shed, by painting or siting it in an imaginative way (*see p.29*).

VEGETABLE ARCH
Marrows or squash make a decorative, productive arch. Fruit trees can be trained to create a similar effect.

CLEVER SHED
With its sliding glass cold-frame front, this shed combines storage space with a sheltered place for seedlings.

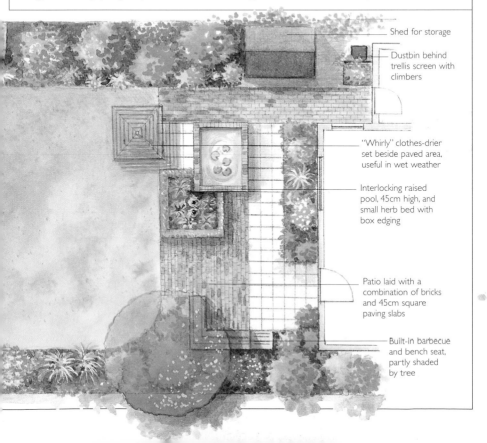

Shed for storage

Dustbin behind trellis screen with climbers

"Whirly" clothes-drier set beside paved area, useful in wet weather

Interlocking raised pool, 45cm high, and small herb bed with box edging

Patio laid with a combination of bricks and 45cm square paving slabs

Built-in barbecue and bench seat, partly shaded by tree

A FORMAL DESIGN

GARDENS IN A FORMAL STYLE impart a feeling of calm and stability – perhaps they bring with them a reminder of the order in monastic gardens. This design, with its use of repeated pattern in the box-edged beds and herringbone brickwork, and its strong central axis, epitomizes the formal look. The style is usually associated with traditional buildings, but it can look dramatic with a modern house, especially if you use unexpected materials (*see p.71*).

DESIGN BRIEF

- Formal-style garden, with strong, symmetrical features.
- Design to give all-year interest.
- Box-edged beds and topiary.
- Secluded, lightly shaded place to sit.
- Planting at rear to screen factory wall.
- Place for existing cast-iron table and chairs.

Four beds, edged in evergreen box (*Buxus sempervirens*), look just as effective in winter. Their topiary cones accentuate the line of the central path

Brick laid in herringbone pattern paves the upper area

Beds contain identical planting patterns of flowering plants

A pair of containers set on low brick pillars flank the steps leading up to the seat

York stone steps lead to a small area with a bench seat, shaded by overhead beams and climbing plants

Raised planting area, with a mixture of medium and large flowering shrubs and climbers on wall, screens neighbouring buildings from view

ELEMENTS OF FORMALITY

Formalism relies heavily on pattern, with beds defined by low, clipped hedges. Box is the plant traditionally used, but a dwarf *Berberis thunbergii*, such as 'Bagatelle', and grey-leaved santolina and lavender can also work well. In the past, beds were filled with coloured gravel, even coal, but today they are more likely to contain flowering or foliage plants. Ornament and furniture styles tend to be classical, such as terracotta pots or stone benches, but in a contemporary design, materials such as metal, glass and plastic can be highly effective. Geometric precision is essential, so work out plans on paper down to the last detail.

SIMPLE SYMMETRY
Topiary, an important ingredient, reinforces the symmetry of this design, with neat cones at the corners of the box hedges, and a pair of bay "pillars" flanking the path to a seat.

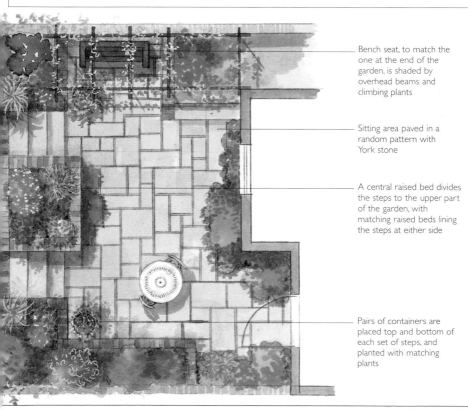

Bench seat, to match the one at the end of the garden, is shaded by overhead beams and climbing plants

Sitting area paved in a random pattern with York stone

A central raised bed divides the steps to the upper part of the garden, with matching raised beds lining the steps at either side

Pairs of containers are placed top and bottom of each set of steps, and planted with matching plants

THE DECKED EFFECT

DECKING IS A GOOD WAY to extend indoor space outside, since it can be installed at floor level without any worries about covering up the damp-proof course. Because it is set on timber joists, decking allows air to circulate and water to drain through. Brush regularly with a stiff broom to stop it from becoming slippery, or apply a special decking paint used on yachts. It comes in pleasing colours and contains a non-slip grit that gives a fine texture.

Raised bed built from old railway sleepers

Small pool is created from an old cast-iron bowl set into the decking

Framed mirror, fixed to the garden wall, reflects the planting opposite (see p.61)

Railway sleepers form an edging to the planting areas and contain the gravel

DESIGN BRIEF

- Low maintenance surface, no lawn.
- Shape of garden to appear as interesting and as large as possible, perhaps using mirrors.
- Raised bed at rear with planting to hide ugly building beyond.
- Built-in dining area with screening to obscure view from neighbour's house.
- Small water feature using old cast-iron bowl.

Framed mirror, set at an angle across the corner, creates the illusion of greater depth

Painted metal screen, which also acts as a support for climbing plants, surrounds the dining area, which has a built-in table and bench seats

Central area of raked gravel. The surface is 15cm below the level of the decking and edging of sleepers

Timber decking, painted pale blue with non-slip paint, is set at an angle of 45° to the house and at the same level as the floor inside

USING WOODEN DECKING

Decking is constructed using the same principles as wooden flooring in a house – planking is nailed or screwed to strong timber supports or joists. It needs to be expertly installed, especially if it adjoins the house; local building regulations may apply. Lay planks with the end-grain rings facing down to avoid curling. Take a timber merchant's advice on materials; for the most part, good quality softwood is adequate provided it has been pressure-treated with preservative. It can then be painted (*see opposite*) or stained in a shade of your choice to improve its weather resistance as well as its finish.

▶ ROUND THE BEND
A versatile material, timber is particularly useful for cutting into shapes to create curving paths. On gently sloping ground it can be stepped.

▼ CHEQUERBOARD FASHION
Ready-made panels can be laid directly on top of coarse gravel that allows drainage underneath. Grooved boards help to stop wood from becoming slippery when wet.

AN ABSTRACT APPROACH

WHETHER YOU LIVE in a traditional or contemporary style house, you may feel you want to do something different. Most designs are based on two-dimensional patterns with a series of interlocking shapes. Here, strong directional spines fan out from the centre of a doorway and are linked by a series of arcs. The design combines the clean-cut look of some modern materials with plant foliage, and the pattern created can be viewed as an abstract painting.

Stainless steel bench seat, kept cool by the shade of the tree, is curved to match line of the bricks

Obelisk, 1.2m tall, made from wood and given a stone-effect paint finish

Blue-black engineering bricks, set on edge to form a pattern of arcs and act as an edging for the gravel

Sunken pools have stylized ceramic and stainless steel sculptures of a bird and a fish (right-hand pool)

Silvery-grey gravel creates a light, bright surface that contrasts with the greenery of the plants

DESIGN BRIEF

• Unconventional, modern design.

• Gravel surface, using a pale, light-reflecting stone.

• A water feature.

• Some unusual decorative features such as sculpture.

• Bench seat in the shade of a tree.

• All-year interest, with some evergreen plants.

Mixed planting including plenty of shrubs with bold foliage, many of them evergreen

Birch tree, *Betula utilis* var. *jacquemontii*, with dazzling white bark

Wall painted a pale colour so that it, too, reflects light. Climbing plants trained against it create a decorative pattern

Patches of clipped box (*Buxus sempervirens*), kept to 30–40cm high

Black, highly polished fibreglass used to create arcs and edging to the two pools

USING INNOVATIVE MATERIALS

A striking design calls for the adventurous use of materials. The plan opposite features a stainless steel sculpture, sleek edgings of polished fibreglass and an obelisk painted to look like stone. You can introduce unexpected textures and colour in furniture and garden structures – glass blocks, rope, canvas and sheets of Perspex (a drawback with some may be that with the long-term effects of weather and pollution they will need regular cleaning). Glass nuggets (a by-product of recyling bottles) make a good mulch. Architectural salvage yards are an excellent hunting ground for all manner of objects that can be converted into alternative sculptures or put to practical use for paths, edgings, screens and containers.

◀ LUSTROUS PATH
The gleam of glazed ceramic balls, set in cement to make a pathway, is accentuated by an edging of shingle.

▼ TRANSPARENT WALL
Glass blocks create an unusual screen, and galvanized metal bins can be used as planters. Drill drainage holes in any improvised containers.

BASIC DESIGN TECHNIQUES

TAKING ACCURATE measurements and drawing a plan to scale may at first seem time-consuming, but using the following techniques helps to ensure that your design works and is easily transferred to the garden. First make a survey, then a base plan (*p.75*) and, when you have completed your design, a setting-out plan (*p.77*). This is then marked on the ground using sand, giving you a chance to see that it looks right and to make any necessary adjustments.

HOW TO MAKE A SURVEY

Before starting to work out a design, you need to make a simple survey of what exists, including details of the side of the house facing the garden. This enables you to draw up the basic plan at a convenient scale. It is worth investing in an architect's scale rule, which gives you the most commonly used scales of 1:50 and 1:100. Once you have the basic plan, you can then start to draw up the overall design, taking into account everything you wish to retain, such as trees and sheds. To make a survey you need a 30m and a 3m measuring tape, a clipboard, some sheets of paper and a sharp pencil. Before measuring, make a clear, free-hand sketch of what exists, starting with the house and any other buildings such as sheds, marking in all windows and doors. Then fill in all the measurements, including windows and doors. The sketch plan below (the survey for the design on p.64) shows how to lay down the tape and take "running dimensions", taking in all the features including the existing planting.

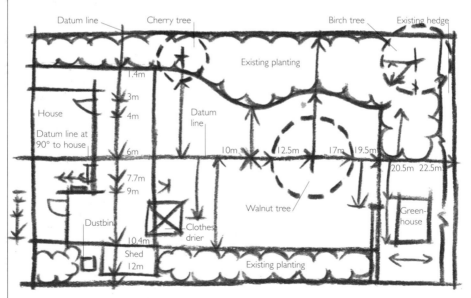

SURVEY SKETCH *Establish two datum lines for taking the first sets of measurements along the garden's length and width (near the house* *for marking door and window sizes). Then take all other measurements (indicated by arrows) including buildings, trees and borders.*

Pinpointing Trees (Triangulation)

An easy way of pinpointing the exact position of trees is to use the method of triangulation. This simply means that when you are doing your survey you take two measurements from the tree's trunk to two fixed points, such as the corners of the house. Make a rough sketch on site, putting in the two measurements, then use compasses to plot the tree's precise position (*see below*), which can then be transferred to the scale plan. Triangulation is a good method to use in a garden with few features.

MARKING A TREE
Make a sketch with the two measurements from house to tree. Draw the house to scale, then take a pair of compasses and draw two arcs, using the two measurements as the radii, from the two corners of the house. The point where the two arcs cross marks the tree's exact position in relation to the house.

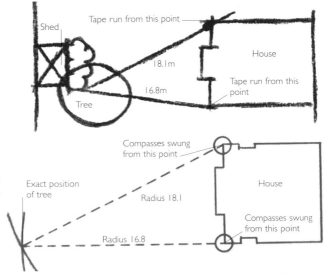

Shed

Tape run from this point

House

18.1m

16.8m

Tape run from this point

Tree

Compasses swung from this point

Exact position of tree

Radius 18.1

House

Radius 16.8

Compasses swung from this point

Dealing with Odd-shaped Boundaries

Triangulation can also be used to determine the point at which two boundaries meet. This is especially useful if you have an odd-shaped garden, such as the plan on page 48, where triangulation will give the exact position of the far corner. The principle is the same. Take two measurements from the point in question to two fixed points on the house, such as the corners, and use compasses (*see above*) to plot it exactly.

MARKING A BOUNDARY
Take two measurements (x and y and a and b) from each corner of the garden to the fixed points on the house. Then transfer them to your scale plan, using a pair of compasses, as above.

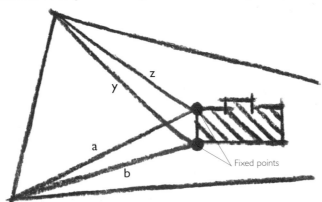

z

y

a

b

Fixed points

CALCULATING SLOPES

If your garden slopes, you will need to determine the degree and whether the slope runs from back to front or from side to side, or whether there is a cross-fall with the slope running from one corner to another. For most small gardens, it is possible to estimate the amount of slope using simple techniques (*see right*). If not, use the method shown below.

SOME EASY METHODS

- If there is a wall, count the difference in the number of brick courses over a given distance.
- With standard fencing panels, measure each stepped rise or drop along the fence's length.
- Select a fixed level, e.g. a manhole cover, for a datum. Relate all other levels plus or minus to this datum level.

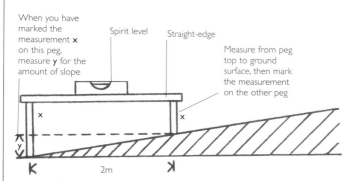

When you have marked the measurement **x** on this peg, measure **y** for the amount of slope

Spirit level

Straight-edge

Measure from peg top to ground surface, then mark the measurement on the other peg

2m

MEASURING A SLOPE
Knock two pegs into the ground and lay a straight-edge and spirit level across. The depth of y *gives you the amount of slope, in this example in a distance of 2m. You may need to take a series of measurements like this across the garden.*

ALLOWING FOR THE UTILITIES

It is all too easy to ignore what is going on underground in the garden – where the services such as water, gas and electricity come into the house, and how the pattern of drainage works. But knowing where they all lie is especially important if you want to dig down to build a water feature, or if you are creating sunken areas of paving that will require draining. Check any information given on house deeds and note where pipes enter the house to help ascertain their route below ground level.

DOWN THE DRAIN
By looking at manhole covers and down pipes, you can quite often work out the drainage pattern. Sometimes it is necessary to lift the covers and pour buckets of water down gulleys to determine the depth of the drains and what is going where in which direction. This diagram shows the sort of pattern you might find.

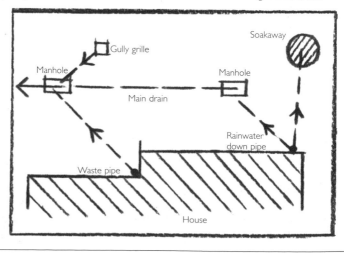

Gully grille

Soakaway

Manhole

Manhole

Main drain

Rainwater down pipe

Waste pipe

House

DRAWING UP THE PLAN

When the survey is complete and everything has been measured and noted, you need to decide what you want to retain and what you want to change. For instance, decide whether you want to keep existing trees and shrubs. The rough plan below is based on the survey on page 72 and shows the features to be retained. It is also useful to mark aspects of the site (see the checklist below) that will affect your design. You can then transfer this information to a scale drawing by overlaying it with a scale grid, plotting it on graph paper or drawing it out using a scale rule. This will act as the base plan for your design, where you can introduce all the new elements. Show the position of all windows and doorways, as these can have an important influence.

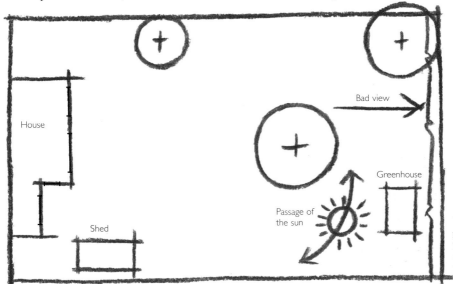

House

Bad view

Greenhouse

Passage of
the sun

Shed

MAKING THE BASE PLAN
The survey and rough plan (above), showing the features to be retained, are used to draw a base plan to scale. Mark the dimensions of all house doors and windows, the direction of the sun and prevailing winds (if these are likely to cause a problem), good views and bad views and, where necessary, other items on the checklist (right). You might find it useful to overlay the plan with tracing paper to try different design ideas. This plan was used in designing the garden on p.64.

DESIGN CHECKLIST

Before you start to work out your design, make sure that you have all the information you need about the various aspects that will affect it. These include:

• Direction of the sun.

• Direction of prevailing winds.

• Good views and bad views.

• Shadows cast by neighbours' trees or surrounding buildings.

• Position of existing trees and buildings, such as shed and greenhouse.

• Degree and direction of any slopes in the garden.

• Pattern of drainage.

• Position underground of gas and electrical services coming into the house.

• Exact level of the house damp-proof course (paving needs to be 15cm below it).

SETTING OUT THE FINISHED DESIGN

Once you are happy with your design, you can draw up a setting-out plan (*see opposite*) to use for transferring the design to the garden. First mark the outline of the design on the ground using soft sand (it helps if the sand is dry) and decide if you want to make any adjustments.

When setting out, it is important to follow a logical sequence, usually starting from the house and working outwards into the garden. Where you are working on more than one level, it often helps to set out and complete the work on the first level (closest to the house) before moving on to the next. (If you are planning to put a design into practice over a period of time, drawing up a work schedule is particularly important. Some features that are to be built at a later stage, for instance, may need electricity for lighting or to work a pump in a pool.)

The following sequence would be the ideal to work to if you were using the setting-out plan on the opposite page.

SEQUENCE OF SETTING OUT

1 Run out a centre line the full length of the garden (it can be done in stages in a split-level garden). Use a builder's square to ensure that it is at right angles to the house and in the middle of the French windows. (Don't take a short cut by running the line from the centre of the back boundary to the house, as this could easily skew the design.) Always work from the centre line.

2 Set out the paving area, working in multiples of 45cm square – the size of the paving slabs specified in the design, allowing for them to be butt-jointed and equally spaced either side of the centre line. You can lay the slabs on the ground (without mortaring) to check the position of the retaining walls.

3 Set out the steps and the retaining walls for the two beds either side of the steps. Check that they look right. Adjust if necessary.

4 Complete work on the paving, retaining walls and steps.

5 In a split-level garden like this, run out the centre line again following the centre of the steps.

6 Measure the centre point for the radius of the lawn. With a string line looped over a centre peg, use a cane (*see below*) to inscribe the line for the edge of the lawn. Mark with soft sand.

7 Measure the centre point of the sundial circle and scribe round and mark with soft sand.

8 Check that both circles fit and that the borders for planting are big enough. Adjust the size of the circles if necessary.

9 Complete the brick circles, prepare and infill with turf and gravel respectively.

10 Prepare the planting areas and put in the plants.

MARKING OUT CURVES

A design will look immeasurably better, much stronger, if you use accurate curves based on circles rather than vague wavy lines. The design will also be easier to set out. To mark a curve, measure to the centre of the circle and knock in a peg. Loop a line over the peg. Measure the radius of the circle along the line and attach a short piece of cane. Keeping the line taut, use the cane to inscribe or scratch in the soil whichever part of the circle's circumference is needed. Then sprinkle a thin band of soft sand all along the mark.

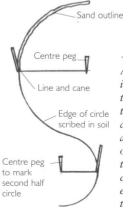

Sand outline

Centre peg

Line and cane

Edge of circle scribed in soil

Centre peg to mark second half circle

◀ LINKING CURVES
A curved line like this is best formed from two half circles joined together. Base your design on true circles and, when setting out, simply measure to the centre of each circle and mark its edge with a cane, then sand.

THE SETTING-OUT PLAN

Once the design is complete, trace off a simple outline plan with all the necessary dimensions for setting it out on the ground. This is a simple setting-out plan for the garden on page 34. When drawing the plan, put yourself in the place of the person who will be doing the work – yourself or a landscape contractor – and think about the order and methods to be used. Here, the size of the butt-jointed paving squares determines the position of the steps and the retaining wall. The centres of circles used to mark curves are also marked. Most importantly, everything is set equally about the centre line, which is set square to the house and runs the length of the garden from the centre of the French windows. Use a builder's square to ensure that the line is at right angles to the house. If you don't have a large builder's square, you can often get one from a hire shop, or make one yourself from some 5×5cm wood.

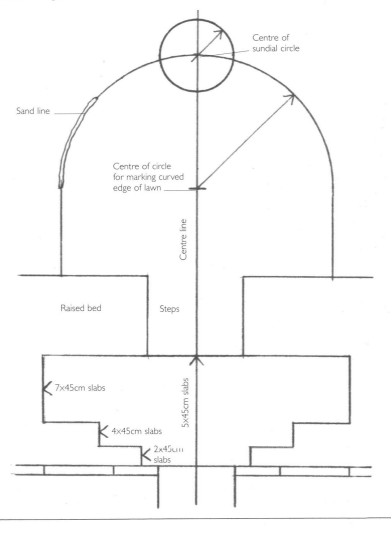

Centre of
sundial circle

Sand line

Centre of circle
for marking curved
edge of lawn

Centre line

Raised bed   Steps

7×45cm slabs

5×45cm slabs

4×45cm slabs

2×45cm
slabs

INDEX